The NCTE Chalkface Series

Literary Terms: A Practical Glossary (1999), Brian Moon

Reading Hamlet (1999), Bronwyn Mellor

Studying Literature: New Approaches to Poetry and Fiction (2000), Brian Moon

Reading Stories: Activities and Texts for Critical Readings (2000), Bronwyn Mellor, Marnie O'Neill, and Annette Patterson

Reading Fictions: Applying Literary Theory to Short Stories (2000), Bronwyn Mellor, Annette Patterson, and Marnie O'Neill

Gendered Fictions (2000), Wayne Martino with Bronwyn Mellor

Investigating Texts: Analyzing Fiction and Nonfiction in High School (2001), Bronwyn Mellor and Annette Patterson

Studying Poetry: Activities, Resources, and Texts (2001), Brian Moon

Bronwyn Mellor
Annette Patterson
Marnie O'Neill

Reading Fictions

Applying Literary Theory to Short Stories

National Council of Teachers of English
1111 W. Kenyon Road, Urbana, Illinois 61801-1096

Editor at Chalkface Press: Brian Moon

NCTE Staff Editor: Tom Tiller

Interior Design: Richard Maul

Cover Design: Pat Mayer

Permissions: Kim Black

NCTE Stock Number: 38691-3050

First published in Australia in 1991 by Chalkface Press, P. O. Box 23, Cottesloe 6011, Western Australia.

Library of Congress Cataloging-in-Publication Data
Mellor, Bronwyn.
Reading fictions: applying literary theory to short stories/Bronwyn Mellor, Annette Patterson, Marnie O'Neill.
p. cm. — (The NCTE Chalkface series)
"First published in Australia in 1991 by Chalkface Press"—T.p. verso.
Includes bibliographical references.
ISBN 0-8141-3869-1(pbk.)
1. Short stories, English—Study and teaching. 2. Literature—History and criticism—Theory, etc. 3. Short stories, American—Study and teaching. 4. Short stories. 5. Short story. I. Patterson, Annette Hinman. II. O'Neill, Marnie H. III. Title. IV. Series.
PR829 .M45 2000
823'.01'07—dc21

00-056239

Series Foreword

Twenty years ago we judged the success of our students' responses to a reading assignment by the similarity of their responses to a text with ours. We saw it as our job to help students read well, to read with understanding, to read correctly; in other words, we did our best to make students read as we read. We gave little thought to the processes and experiences at work that make a single reading of a text impossible and often even undesirable. We learn much, thank goodness, as we teach. By now we have learned to encourage our students to read diversely, to recognize the processes interplaying and influencing their readings, to examine the cultural factors influencing and the cultural consequences resulting from their reading practices.

Moving beyond encouragement to effective, integrated instruction and practice is always difficult. That is why we are so excited about the NCTE Chalkface Series. Never before have we seen such practical methods of examining and understanding the personal and cultural influences that affect students' reading. The lessons actively engage students and make the invisible processes of reading explicit, demystify responses to literature, and help students understand the myriad factors influencing their reading. These books, like no other secondary reading texts we have come across, had us seeking out colleagues to share our excitement about published lessons. We now do so at every opportunity.

Among the specific strengths in the books are the inclusion of theory and of questions that provide the basis for the applications/student practices. For example, in *Literary Terms: A Practical Glossary,* the study of each term is developed as a minilesson, including a short piece to help students with mind-set, a brief theoretical explanation, an activity that requires application, and a summary. Some terms are very common, such as *author* and *character;* others are less common, such as *polysemy* and *poststructuralism*. The material is student-accessible; the format is somewhat different from the traditional glossaries of literary terms. Students and teachers should find the activities very useful illustrations of the terms' definitions and the theories that serve as the foundations of the study of literature.

Gendered Fictions, another title in the series, operates essentially from the premise that texts offer differing "versions of reality" rather than a single illustration of the real world. The authors contend that we are conditioned to make sense of text by reading from a gendered position. They offer many opportunities for students to accept or challenge particular ways of looking at masculinity or femininity. A major question proposed by the text is *how* readers read—a critical question if we want our students to be analytical readers. Perhaps equally basic, the text encourages students to look at how they become what they become. As is true of the other books, the approach is not didactic. Questioning, yes; deterministic, no.

Reading Fictions follows similar assumptions: texts do not have a single, definitive meaning; rather, meaning depends on a number of variables. The authors do suggest that a text may very well have a *dominant* reading (i.e., what a majority of readers may agree is there), but it may also have *alternative* readings (i.e., what other readers may believe is there). The intent is to have students look at various texts and consider what may be a dominant reading or an alternative reading. Again, the intent is to facilitate skill, not to determine what students should believe.

Reading Hamlet positions *Hamlet* as a revenge tragedy and provides students with a context by offering a brief look at other revenge tragedies of roughly the same period: *Thyestes, Gorboduc, The Spanish Tragedy,* and *Titus Andronicus*. That may sound overwhelming; it is, rather, illustrative and offers a genuinely effective context for the study of *Hamlet*. The text also offers a number of ways for students to study character as well as opportunities for student performance. The performance component, in particular, gives students the opportunity to be actively involved with text. The author does not assume that students have to be talented actors.

Studying Poetry again offers opportunities for student performance, considerations of what poetry is, and exercise in writing critiques of poetry. Poems chosen for study range from traditional to contemporary. The book strongly encourages students to identify their own favorite poems, a practice also promoted by America's current poet laureate, Robert Pinsky.

Studying Literature goes to the fundamental question of what makes a piece of writing "literature," asking students to consider features of writing along with their own beliefs and values and encouraging them to reflect critically on the nature of the activity in which they are engaged rather than merely engaging in it.

Reading Stories lays a firm foundation for students moving toward becoming critical readers. From exploring their own expectations prior to reading a work (or rereading one) to questioning authorial intent to exploring cultural and social assumptions, this book makes explicit both the ways in which readings are constructed and the bases on which students might choose among them.

Investigating Texts builds on that foundation by exploring the deeper questions of how texts are made, how ways of reading change, and how texts can be read differently. As in all the books, numerous activities are provided to facilitate such exploration and application, promoting student interaction, an active relationship with the texts provided and, by extension, an active relationship with new texts they encounter.

We are delighted that NCTE has arranged to make Chalkface books available to its members. We are confident that teachers will share our enthusiasm for the publications.

Richard Luckert
Olathe East High School
Olathe, Kansas

William G. McBride
Colorado State University
Fort Collins

Contents

Acknowledgments

We thank the following for their help in the development of this book: Lynne Carew, Peter Forrestal, Betty Johnson, Jo-Anne Reid, and Andrew Sooby. Alison Lee very generously spent time proofreading the manuscript and made many useful comments. We also thank Brian Moon for his careful, thoughtful editing and his many productive suggestions.

We are grateful to Lyn Dale, Elaine Forrestal, Barbara North, and Ann Sankey for typing the manuscript.

Permissions

Grateful acknowledgment is made to the following publishers and individuals for granting permission to reprint material in this book.

"A Blow, a Kiss" by Tim Winton, reprinted with permission of the author from *Scission and Other Stories,* first published in 1985 by McPhee Gribble Publishers.

"Debut" by Kristin Hunter, from *Guests in the Promised Land* by Kristin Hunter. Copyright 1968 Avon Books. Reprinted by permission.

"How I Contemplated the World from the Detroit House of Correction and Began My Life Over Again" by Joyce Carol Oates, copyright by The Ontario Review, Inc., 1993, from *Where Are You Going, Where Have You Been?* (Ontario Review Press, 1993). Reprinted with permission.

"Looking for a Rain God" by Bessie Head, from *"The Collector of Treasures" and Other Botswana Village Tales* by Bessie Head (Heinemann, 1977). © Bessie Head 1977. Reprinted with permission.

"A Lot to Learn" by Robert T. Kurosaka, from *The Little Book of Horrors: Tiny Tales of Terror,* edited by Sebastian Wolfe, published by arrangement with Barricade Books, NY, www.Barricade.net. Reprinted by permission of Barricade Books.

"The Lottery" by Marjorie Faith Barnard, reprinted by permission of the copyright owner, Curtis Brown (Australia), Sydney.

"Manhood" by John Wain reproduced with permission of Curtis Brown Ltd., London, on behalf of the estate of John Wain. Copyright John Wain 1966.

"The Scarlatti Tilt" by Richard Brautigan, from *Revenge of the Lawn.* Copyright 1963, 1964, 1965, 1966, 1967, 1969, 1970, 1971 by Richard Brautigan. Reprinted by permission of Houghton Mifflin Co. All rights reserved.

"The Test" by Angelica Gibbs, copyright Angelica Gibbs, reprinted with permission.

"A Way of Talking" by Patricia Grace, from *Waiariki and Other Stories* by Patricia Grace, Longman Paul New Zealand (now Pearson Education New Zealand Limited), 1975. Reprinted with permission of the publisher.

Preface

To Students

This book is about texts—in this case, stories—and how you read them.

As a reader, you probably have available to you *readings* or interpretations of most of the stories in this anthology already—that is, even before you read them. For example, you probably can predict quite a lot about the kinds of stories which might follow from these summaries:

- a story about a scientist who invents a machine that will supply anything requested;
- a story about a young woman who is afraid someone is watching her;
- a story about a fifteen-year-old girl who runs away from her rich family's luxurious home to the mean streets of the city;
- a story about a surfer who is saved by a girl from drowning;
- a story of a drought and the lengths to which people will go to make it rain.

This book, however, does not focus only on *what* stories might be about, but also on *how* they mean, and *why* they are often made to mean in quite different ways by different groups of readers.

Texts in this book are not thought of as containing meanings. We argue instead that reading *produces* possible meanings of a text, and that they are always plural. What is more, it is claimed that there can never be only one final reading of a text, because there is no possibility of a neutral or objective judge to decide which reading or meaning is correct.

Texts are described as incomplete and fragmentary. It may seem as if all the meaning is in "the words on the page," but this is because readers have learned to produce detailed readings from only bits of text, or textual fragments, by filling gaps between fragments.

Rather than considering that there are "correct" readings of texts, we argue that there are dominant readings. These are sets of meanings which certain groups in a society agree about. Other readings which disagree with the dominant readings of texts are described as alternative or resistant readings.

In writing and reading texts, then, writers and readers are seen as supporting particular values and disqualifying others. There are, therefore, no neutral or objective readings or texts: not even *Reading Fictions*!

As summarized here, these are complex ideas, but you may find this page useful to refer to as you work through the activities in this book, which are designed to help you analyze possible readings of the short stories in this collection.

To the Teacher

At the beginning of each of the six chapters in *Reading Fictions,* there is a brief introduction to some of the ideas that recent literary theory suggests about reading, readers, and texts. The subsequent activities accompanying the two short stories in each chapter are intended to help explicate these sometimes quite difficult concepts for students.

The six chapters are designed to offer a cumulative learning experience; each introduces a range of terms and concepts which build on the previous chapter's work. It is suggested that the sections be covered in sequence, although the emphasis that teachers decide to give to the various chapters may vary.

Many of the activities are planned for pairs or small groups, which may then lead to class discussion. Since many of the concepts presented in the book are quite complex and may be unfamiliar to students, we have deliberately developed a number of activities such as prediction, chart building, and comparative analysis. We see these as a means of drawing attention to the contradictions, gaps, and silences of texts, and of defamiliarizing those aspects of texts which contribute to an apparent seamlessness or "neutrality." Your students may be able to come to terms with abstractions without working through all of the activities; you may want to leave some things out, or substitute others that will achieve the same objectives in ways more appropriate to your students. Obviously, different classes work in different ways, and you will want to vary the proportion of individual, small-group, and whole-class activities to suit your students.

In cases where predictions are used to help students analyze their readings, it will be worthwhile considering how to present the stories in ways that encourage students to give adequate time to the suggested activities before continuing reading.

By working through the chapters in this book, students, we hope, will be able to consider different possible readings of the texts. However, we are not arguing here simply for a plurality of readings or interpretations based on the personal experience of readers. Rather, we hope that the activities accompanying each short story will encourage and enable students to:

- analyze how they produce particular readings;
- consider what is at stake in the differences between competing readings;
- ask on whose behalf particular readings are made.

1 Texts and Readings

In the past, texts were often thought about as if they were a kind of container. Inside the containers were meanings. Readers looked, sometimes quite hard, to find the meanings in the containers. "Reading" meant finding the "correct" meaning in each container, or text.

Recent literary theory, however, argues that texts are not containers with meanings "inside" them. Instead, texts are seen as *polysemic* or "multi-meaninged." Reading, it is argued, *produces* the meanings of a text, which, in this book, are called *readings.*

Because texts are full of *gaps,* they can be read in different ways, and it is not possible to decide finally "what a text means." A text can never be reduced to a single meaning, because there is no possibility of a neutral authority or judge to decide which reading is "correct."

This doesn't imply that a text can mean anything a reader likes. In theory, texts have the potential to be read in endlessly different ways, but in practice, groups of readers produce a limited range of meanings, by valuing certain responses and disqualifying others.

These ideas change what might be asked about the reading of texts. Instead of asking, "What does this text mean?" it is important to ask:

- *How* does this text mean?
- What are possible readings of this text?
- What is at stake in the differences between readings?
- On what basis is it possible to decide between different readings?

"A Lot to Learn"

The story that follows may seem a simple tale. It is short, and the style appears straightforward. The narrative structure probably will be familiar to you and may remind you in quite specific ways of other texts that you have read or seen. Your reading of it, then, may *seem* quite simple too.

This chapter, however, aims to disrupt or challenge the ease and apparent naturalness with which you can read texts similar to this. It is hoped that making reading seem "strange" will enable you to think about how you produce meanings from texts, and for what purposes.

Have You Heard the One about the Scientist?

- Individually, jot down answers to this riddle for later discussion: Why does the scientist, who invents a machine that will supply whatever is requested, ask to be given a member of the opposite sex?

Expectations

- Now, read the beginning of "A Lot to Learn" (below), and then pause to discuss, in your group, the questions indicated before reading the rest of the story.

A Lot to Learn

R. T. Kurosaka

The Materializer was completed.

Ned Quinn stood back, wiped his hands, and admired the huge bank of dials, lights and switches. Several years and many fortunes had gone into this project. Finally it was ready.

Ned placed the metal skullcap on his head and plugged the wires into the control panel. He turned the switch to ON and spoke:

"Pound note."

There was a whirring sound. In the Receiver a piece of paper appeared. Ned inspected it. Real.

"Martini," he said.

A whirring sound. A puddle formed in the Receiver. Ned cursed silently. He had a lot to learn.

"A bottle of beer," he said.

The whirring sound was followed by the appearance of the familiar brown bottle. Ned tasted the contents and grinned.

Chuckling, he experimented further.

Ned enlarged the Receiver and prepared for his greatest experiment. He switched on the Materializer, took a deep breath and said,

"Girl."

The whirring sound swelled and faded. In the Receiver stood a lovely girl. She was naked. Ned had not asked for clothing.

She had freckles, a brace and pigtails. She was eight years old.

Pause here and discuss the following questions:

- What do you think might happen next in the story?
- Where are your expectations "coming from"?

After discussion, read the rest of the story:

> "Hell!" said Quinn.
>
> Whirr.
>
> The fireman found two charred skeletons in the smouldering rubble.

A Riddle?

- As part of a class discussion, draw a diagram of the possible connections between the riddle about the scientist and the story you have just read.

Ned	invention	machine	scientist
Girl	a member of the opposite sex	Materializer	

Asked to make connections between the riddle and the story, most readers are able to do this. But how is this possible? The riddle does not mention the sex of the scientist nor, therefore, the sex of the wished for "opposite." The story, on the other hand, does not refer to Ned as a "scientist."

- If this information is not "on the page," how can readers make connections at all?
- From where do readers produce connections, if not from the page?
- What similarities and differences were there in the assumptions made in your class about connections between the riddle and the story?

One Reading?

- Below is a list of readings of "A Lot to Learn." With a partner, discuss each one, in terms of whether it is a "reasonable" reading or not. Indicate *yes, no,* or *maybe,* and make brief notes in support of your decisions.

"A Lot to Learn" is:

1. a skillfully constructed science fiction text;
2. a modern fairy tale;
3. an apparently antisexist tale;
4. a text that draws attention to the power relationships involved in naming;
5. a lighthearted spoof of a familiar kind of science fiction story;
6. a story that plays with the conventions of the fairy tale and science fiction genres;
7. a powerful condemnation of Ned's sexist attitude towards women;
8. disturbingly sexist in its presentation of the death of the girl as incidental;
9. a witty and humorous send-up of masculine fantasies;
10. a humorous example of the difficulties of communication.

How Might Each of These Readings Have Been Produced?

It used to be thought that readers simply read what was "in the text." Recently, however, it has been argued that acts of reading *produce* the meanings of a text.

Texts are not seen as consistent or complete. Instead, it is suggested that they are *contradictory* and *fragmentary,* and that it is readers who unify and complete them by ignoring or resolving contradictions and filling gaps with meanings available to them in their culture.

An Example

In this extract from "A Lot to Learn," a study of the "moves" readers make from one sentence to the next can highlight gaps which usually remain invisible.

- In your group, spend a few minutes discussing (a) what readers are not explicitly "told" by the text, and (b) what they need to *assume* in order to construct a reading of the following sentences:

Sentences (from the story)	**Gap? (What is the reader not "told" by the text?)**
He switched on the Materializer, took a deep breath and said, "Girl."	
The whirring sound swelled and faded. In the Receiver stood a lovely girl. She was naked. Ned had not asked for clothing.	
She had freckles, a brace and pigtails. She was eight years old.	
"Hell!" said Quinn.	

Readers are not told:

- why Ned asks for a girl;
- what his reaction to her nakedness might be;
- what his reaction to her appearance and her age might be;
- why he says "Hell!"

Readers fill these gaps with already-available ways of thinking about men, women, children, and sex.

Analyzing Different Readings

One way of trying to examine how different readings of a text are made or *constructed* is to analyze each reading in terms of:

- what "bits" of the text or *textual fragments* are emphasized or *foregrounded;*
- what textual fragments are *privileged* or read as most important;
- what textual fragments are ignored, *marginalized,* or *silenced;*
- how particular textual fragments are read to "fit" a reading;
- how gaps are filled.

An Example

To read "A Lot to Learn" as science fiction, for example, you might foreground the scientific vocabulary and read it and the plot as typical of the genre. (Although, is the vocabulary scientific? A "Materializer" *could* be read as a genie. Or, the apparatus could work by magic.)

On the other hand, to read the story as a modern fairy tale, you might emphasize or foreground its similarity to stories of that genre in which wishes are granted. It is usually three wishes that are granted and not four, as in "A Lot to Learn," but you would ignore this.

- In your pair, discuss the following two readings and try to analyze what might be (a) foregrounded and (b) silenced in each of them. See also if you can suggest (c) whether the *same* textual fragments have been read differently and (d) how gaps have been filled. Some ideas are suggested below the chart to get your discussion started.

Reading A "A Lot to Learn" is an apparently antisexist story.	**Reading B** "A Lot to Learn" is a humorous example of the difficulties of communication.
	Silences gender.

Foregrounds the naming of "girl."
Foregrounds the death of the girl.
Ignores the death of the girl.
Fills a particular gap with a humorous reading of the girl/woman confusion.

Foregrounds gender.
Silences gender.
Reads naming in terms of gender.
Fills a particular gap with a feminist reading of the girl/woman confusion.

Correct Readings?

The activities you have worked on may have raised more questions than they have answered about how *you* read "A Lot to Learn" and how it *might* be read. The idea that a "correct" meaning is in a text is hard to defend, and most critics no longer try. There still is disagreement, however, over the reasonableness or *validity of readings.*

It can be argued, for example, that the two readings on the chart just discussed, while very different (and some readers would say contradictory), are both valid readings of "A Lot to Learn." Some critics, however, might try to assert that one of the readings is more reasonable or valid than the other by pointing to what they would argue is "evidence" in the text. The problem is that it is just as possible for other critics or readers to "find" other "evidence," or even to read the *same* "evidence," in support of a quite different reading.

In the remaining part of this chapter, and in the next chapter, you are asked to consider the following questions.

- Where do meanings come from if they are not "on the page"?
- If it is not possible to *authorize,* or guarantee, a particular reading of a text as the correct one by pointing to a fixed meaning *in* the text, then on what basis is it possible to choose among different readings?

Changing Stories

- Read the altered extract below from "A Lot to Learn."

The Materializer was completed.

Nell Quinn stood back, wiped her hands, and admired the huge bank of dials, lights and switches. Several years and many fortunes had gone into this project. Finally it was ready.

Nell placed the metal skullcap on her head and plugged the wires into the control panel. She turned the switch to ON and spoke:

"Pound note."

There was a whirring sound. In the Receiver a piece of paper appeared. Nell inspected it. Real.

"Martini," she said.

A whirring sound. A puddle formed in the Receiver. Nell cursed silently. She had a lot to learn.

"A bottle of beer," she said.

The whirring sound was followed by the appearance of the familiar brown bottle. Nell tasted the contents and grinned.

Chuckling, she experimented further.

Nell enlarged the Receiver and prepared for her greatest experiment. She switched on the Materializer, took a deep breath and said,

"Boy."

The whirring sound swelled and faded. In the Receiver stood a lovely boy. He was naked. Nell had not asked for clothing.

He had freckles, a brace and a crew cut. He was eight years old.

For Discussion

- In your group, discuss how readers might predict Nell Quinn's reaction at this point. How might it be read differently from Ned's?
- Consider how changing Ned to Nell and altering the gender references might affect readings of: (a) the kinds of "wishes" or requests made, (b) the fate of the scientist, and (c) the child and his or her fate.
- In a class discussion, share ideas from your group's talk. Debate to what extent the alterations in names and pronouns produce changes in readings that do not appear to be "on the page."

Reading Masculinity and Femininity

"A Lot to Learn," like all texts, is fragmentary, or composed of bits of text. To produce a reading, readers fill gaps between fragments with ideas and assumptions available to them in their culture.

Changing the gender of the characters appears to alter the ways in which gaps are filled, and the readings that are produced, because different assumptions are made about masculinity and femininity. While readers are usually clear about the reason Ned asks for a "Girl," they are often less decided about why Nell should ask for a "Boy." Some readers suggest she might want a son, but few readers suggest that Ned wants a daughter.

There also appear to be differences in how Ned and Nell are "read" if it is argued that what they both want is a lover. Ned's desire is seen as "natural," while Nell's is frequently seen as morally questionable.

Readings, such as these, cause arguments, not because it matters so much what "Ned" or "Nell" is like, but because such different readings support particular ways of thinking about masculinity and femininity, about how men and women should behave, and about what their respective desires should be.

"Listen to the End"

While reading the next story, "Listen to the End," you are asked to consider:

- how different *reading practices,* or ways of reading, might produce different meanings;
- what is at stake in the disagreements among competing readings;
- on what basis readers might choose among readings.

Different Readings

"Listen to the End," by Tony Hunter, has been read in a number of quite contradictory ways since its first publication in 1981.

After the story, three readings by critics have been printed for you to compare. The first critic reads the story as an exciting entertainment, the second describes it as "nasty" and "prurient," and the last argues that the story should be read simply as a joke.

Expectations

- The opening paragraphs of the story are printed below. Read the excerpt, and then, with a partner, brainstorm as many predictions as possible about the story that you think will follow.

  A flurry of wind sent the brown leaves tumbling end over end ahead of her along the dark, glistening pavement. Thin, cold drizzle, driven by the wind wrapped a clammy embrace round her hurrying figure and swirls of mist danced beckoningly around the street lamps, transmuting their normally friendly beacons into baleful yellow eyes. The tall Victorian houses frowned down disapprovingly on the small figure in the bright red raincoat as if the bright splash of colour offended their staid and sombre tastes.

  She quickened her pace, head bent, dark hair plastered damply across a pale face, heels beating out a staccato rhythm that took off with the promise of an echo only to be swallowed by the all-pervading mist, thickening now as it rolled up from the river. The paper bag of groceries, dampened by mist and rain, threatened once more to disgorge its contents and she shifted the grip of her arms, clutching it even more tightly to her breast carrying it before her like a shield against the dark.

  Not far now, she told herself. Then home, out of the cold and wet into the warmth and familiarity of the flat. First a hot bath and a long soak, then something to eat and after, with the fire going full blast, an evening spent curled up in an old armchair with a book. She shivered violently and two cans in the bag knocked together, the sound amazingly loud in the cottonwool silence. A pity that her flat mate was away.

- Next, share the results of your brainstorming in a class discussion and comment briefly on what you think it is that has enabled you to make predictions. Then read the full story, presented below.

Listen to the End

Tony Hunter

A flurry of wind sent the brown leaves tumbling end over end ahead of her along the dark, glistening pavement. Thin, cold drizzle, driven by the wind, wrapped a clammy embrace round her hurrying figure, and swirls of mist danced beckoningly around the street lamps, transmuting their normally friendly beacons into baleful yellow eyes. The tall Victorian houses frowned down disapprovingly on the small figure in the bright red raincoat as if the bright splash of colour offended their staid and sombre tastes.

She quickened her pace, head bent, dark hair plastered damply across a pale face, heels beating out a staccato rhythm that took off with the promise of an echo only to be swallowed by the all-pervading mist, thickening now as it rolled up from the river. The paper bag of groceries, dampened by mist and rain, threatened once more to disgorge its contents, and she shifted the grip of her arms, clutching it even more tightly to her breast, carrying it before her like a shield against the dark.

Not far now, she told herself. Then home, out of the cold and wet into the warmth and familiarity of the flat. First a hot bath and a long soak, then something to eat and after, with the fire going full blast, an evening spent curled up in the old armchair with a book. She shivered violently and the two cans in the bag knocked together, the sound amazingly loud in the cottonwool silence. A pity that her flat mate was away. The other girl's non-stop chatter and lighthearted approach to everything, annoying at times, would have been a welcome counter to her present mood. The undemanding routine of a typing pool followed by a swaying lurching train journey, packed shoulder to shoulder in a phalanx of blank-faced commuters all exuding an aura of dampness and defeat and finally the lonely walk through damp, swirling greyness, had combined to drown her spirits in a remorseless, confidence-sapping quagmire. At least, she thought, searching for a cheerful note, I can put on some music, turn on the lights and shut out the grim grey world.

The steps of the house loomed out of the mist and she hurried up them digging awkwardly in her handbag for the key to the brass-knockered front door. It swung open onto the dark, lino-smelling hallway. The rain had stopped, the wind had died away and everything inside and out was very, very still. She steeled herself for the part she hated most about coming home at night. The six steps across the lobby to the foot of the stairs and the frantic groping for the light switch, a little plastic knob that when pressed in activated the stairway lights. Its spring-loaded mechanism, set by a money-conscious landlord, then inched its way out giving you enough time to dash to the first floor and press the next button before being plunged into darkness again. Sometimes her hand would miss the button and there would follow a frantic groping lasting probably only a second, but seeming to go on for eternity while the dark crowded in and the panic stirred within her. Maybe the switch had been moved or even removed completely or maybe she had entered the wrong house and when she turned to the door she would find a stranger standing there. Then her frantic fingers would find the switch and the fears would vanish in the blessed light. But her hand would shake as she grasped the bannister rail.

She stepped across the lobby, hand out in front like a blind person, and thankfully found the switch at the first attempt. Lights blazed on and she clattered quickly up the stairs to the next switch, repeating the process on each landing before reaching the door of the third floor flat. Clutching the bag high, she got her key into the lock and nudged the door open with her shoulder. Flicking on the hall light she closed the door, kicked off her sodden shoes and padded down the hall to the kitchen. Dumping the fast-collapsing bag on the table, she went back down the hall to the lounge door halfway along. Reaching around the door, her fingers found the light switch and pressed it down. The globe in the ceiling gave off a sharp crack, flooded the room with a photographic flash of light and expired.

"Damn," she muttered. No spare globes either. Something she had meant to get but had forgotten during her hurried lunch hour shopping. She was halfway across the room, reaching for the table lamp when the realisation of something half seen in that split second of brilliance caused her heart to lurch sickeningly and her breath to catch in her throat. Something, a suggestion of movement, a fleeting disturbance at the extreme edge of her vision. So tenuous that mind and eye had all but failed to register it and only now picked it up on a re-run of a mental filmstrip. She forced herself to keep walking, anxious now for light again, suppressing a cry of pain as she cracked her shin on the coffee table. Her hand collided with the table lamp nearly dislodging it. She grabbed frantically, fumbled for the switch and as the light came on glanced fearfully across the room. The floor length curtains stirred gently and she saw that the big sash window was fractionally open. She let out a sigh of relief and realised that she had been holding her breath. Crossing quickly she closed the window and pulled the curtains across. As she did so she saw that the fog had thickened to the point where the glow of the street lamp was barely perceptible. She shivered and a droplet of water escaped from her hair and trickled down her neck. Still wearing her raincoat she went back to the kitchen and, removing the dripping garment, hung it on the back of the door. Down the hall to the bathroom where she set the taps running to fill a steaming hot bath. Then through the lounge to her bedroom where she stripped off her clothes, putting the skirt on a hanger and dropping shirt and underwear into the linen basket. Sitting at the dressing table she began to brush out the tangles in her rain soaked hair. After brushing for a minute or so she became aware of a coolness in the air that had not been there before. Almost, but not quite, as if she could physically feel the temperature dropping. Must be the filthy weather she thought. Laying down the brush she walked into the lounge and switched the electric fire onto its highest setting. As she stood before it a little whisper of cold air, no more than the faintest suggestion of coolness, brushed her back. So unexpected was it that its icy kiss induced a long shudder right through her. Goose bumps sprang up all over and her nipples stiffened and became erect. The old house often produced strange draughts. She was used to them, though this one seemed to have a presence rather more marked than most. In the same way the house had quite a repertoire of noises; creaks, groans, knocking sounds, even strange whisperings if you had a good enough imagination. Tonight though, it was strangely silent almost as though the blanket of fog had deadened everything around it. In fact, she thought, the silence was so intense that you could almost feel everything holding its breath. With a start she realised that she was doing so too and feeling rather foolish let it out with a sigh and turned to re-enter the bedroom.

As she turned, an impression, a feeling so intense that it flashed across her mind with the clarity of a neon sign, of not being alone, stopped her movement. The hairs prickled on the nape of her neck and so certain was the feeling that she was being observed that, in an unconscious gesture of femininity, she folded one arm across her breasts while the other hand dropped to her belly. The feeling, which lasted perhaps a millisecond, was so strong that for that moment she knew that if she had turned a fraction quicker, she would have glimpsed the face of her observer. Still she stood for a second more, frozen in naked vulnerability while her heart thudded against her chest. Then the moment passed and with it the feeling. Control took over and the logic of a twentieth century mind asserted itself.

"Hey, come on," she told herself in a voice that carried rather less conviction than she would have liked. "This weather and this house is really giving you the creeps. You'll be hearing rattling chains soon."

She wished she hadn't said that. It somehow seemed, in the old house with its high ceilings and faded paintwork, not so improbable.

"And stop talking to yourself," smiling at the contradiction in words and actions.

She walked resolutely into the bedroom. Donning a robe she made her way to the kitchen and getting out the casserole, prepared the night before, put it to cook in the oven.

The bath was full to just the right level now and dropping the robe to the floor she slid thankfully into the hot scented water. Humming to herself she luxuriated in the steamy embrace, eyes closed, limbs floating, drifting through a drowsy world of half-formed thoughts.

The touch, icy cold across her breasts, shocked her to full consciousness with a savagery that jerked her upright in the bath, water slopping in waves over the side. Her eyes, wide and staring, saw or thought they saw a flicker of shadow at the slightly open bathroom door. The fleeting impression, like the last, had not form or substance but was none the less vivid for that. Then, as she gulped back the cry that had risen to her lips she heard the sound. Seeming to come from all around, from the fabric of the house itself, soft yet insistent, a long drawn-out sigh, deep noted, fading gradually like the dying breath of a dying man. It was a sound filled with longing, with a sense of something unfulfilled but carrying a promise of realisation. Above all, it carried the taint of evil. As the sound faded, the returning silence pressed in with an almost physical weight.

Rigid with fear, her straining hands gripping the edge of the bath she fought back the rising panic that threatened to engulf her reason. Drawing a long shuddering breath and relaxing her grip she reached for the robe. Moving quickly, anxious now to cover her nakedness, she stood and shrugged into it, belting it tightly around her waist. She took a step toward the door and froze again, as silently, inexorably, it swung closed and latched with a tiny metallic click.

Her control snapped then. With a strangled sob she flung herself at the door and wrenched it open, catapulting herself into the hall so violently that she stumbled against the far wall. Breath coming in great heaving gasps she stared around wildly. Nothing. Cream-coloured walls stretched silently away and the solid bulk of the front door stared unwaveringly back.

Behind her. Movement, sensed, not heard. She spun, pressing up against the wall. Again nothing. No. Not there, the other way, from the lounge. Her head jerked from side to side, seeking, like an animal at bay. Again the sigh, stronger, closer, from all around. That breath of cold air again, caressing her neck and she arched away from it, every nerve at snapping point. With a white-knuckled fist thrust against her mouth she stumbled wildly down the hall, the robe now loosened and flying away from her, her free hand slashing the air in front as if to clear a path through a jungle of unseen horror. And as she ran, the walls crowded in and the fingers of ice plucked at her passing figure. She lurched into the lounge and stood, trembling violently, in the middle of the room.

The shattering, strident jangle of the telephone crashed through her whirling brain like a death knell and blood oozed from her knuckles as her teeth clenched in a galvanic reaction. Then the source of the sound registered and with a half cry, half sob she sank to her knees and snatched at the instrument, knocking it from the table. Scrabbling frantically on the floor she grabbed the handset.

"Hi there, sweetheart. What are you doing? Breaking up all the crockery?" The well-loved voice, calm, reassuring and confident filled her with such overwhelming relief that she almost passed out. Fighting back the blackness in front of her eyes she forced her lips to form words.

"P-Please, oh God—thank God," she sobbed. "Help me—please—for God's sake—help me."

"Darling, what the hell's going on?" The voice filled with anxiety now. "What is it? What's happened?"

Her voice was racked with sobs.

"I'm scared. There's something . . . something odd. Cold. Someone. Something here. Not alone. I can feel it." Tears streaming down her face, she blurted out disjointed fragments, almost incoherent with terror.

He forced his voice to remain calm.

"Darling, listen. Get a hold. Breathe deep. Now, tell me quietly. Are you hurt and what's got you in this state?"

His voice cut through the panic and she fought to control her words. Slowly, in a shaking voice, she pieced the sentences together.

"It's just that I've got this . . . this feeling. So strong, that I'm not alone. It's like, well . . . like," she paused, sniffing away the tears, "there's someone watching me. A presence, someone, is close but I can't see them. But I know, I can feel it." Her voice rose again. "When I look . . . I look and it's as though they've been there just before but I'm always too late to see them. And it's cold. When it's there, it's cold."

He resisted the impulse to tell her she was imagining things. She undoubtedly was but he sensed the rising flood of hysteria in her voice and knew she wasn't far from going over the edge into blind panic.

"OK darling. You sit tight. I'm on my way over. Be with you in . . ."

"No, no," she broke in frantically. "Please. I can't just wait here. I don't want to be here. Even for a little while, with no one."

She was close, very close, to breaking now. One little push was all it would take.

"Right." He made his voice clipped, incisive. Something for her to hold fast to. To obey. "This is what you do. Grab a bag. Throw in what you need for tonight, I'll sit here on the phone and you lay your receiver on the table. That way I can hear you moving about and you can call out to me as you get organised. When you're packed, get out of there and walk down to the main street. The pub on the corner. Go in and order yourself the biggest Scotch they sell. Wait for me. Slam the front door good and hard when you leave. When I hear that door close I'll get in the car and head over. Meet you in the pub. Shouldn't be more than fifteen minutes. You can come back and stay at my place. OK? You got all that?"

"Y-Yes." The precise list of instructions and the knowledge that someone was in control had calmed her. "I'll start right now. I'll leave the phone on the coffee table. Then I'll go to the bedroom and get dressed."

"Good girl. Don't forget, I'm right here on the end of the line." He heard the receiver go down and her footsteps recede across the room. Her voice floated back, a little uncertain again now.

"I'm going into the bedroom now. I'm getting dressed."

Silence for a minute. Then a thump as something heavy fell. His heart lurched. Footsteps approached the phone.

"I dropped the bag getting it off the top of the wardrobe," she called shakily.

He relaxed his vice-like grip on the receiver. Heard her moving around again.

"Just getting some things from the bathroom." Footsteps again.

"Nearly ready."

Then her voice, close again.

"OK." She still sounded shaky but in control. "I'm leaving now."

"Don't hang up," he cautioned. "I want to hear that front door slam so I know you're out of there."

"All right. See you soon."

He listened as her footsteps grew fainter. Some interference on the line, a low sighing sound, intruded for a second or two, then faded as he listened for the slam of the front door. He heard instead a click and then the dial tone as the receiver at the other end was gently replaced.

Three Readings

■ Read these extracts from three reviews by critics of "Listen to the End." Then make notes on their differences—and any similarities.

Critic 1

"Listen to the End" is a masterly and entertaining example of the suspense story. With consummate skill, Hunter sets the scene: details of the geographical setting are carefully revealed to hint at a sense of evil and general unease. The young woman's fears seem in comparison, however, almost pedestrian as she struggles through a wet and stormy evening to reach the warmth and security of home.

The details are banal, yet telling; the longing for shelter, for the comfort of a hot bath, for food and drink. Her momentary nervousness in the foyer as she hurries to turn on the light is completely recognisable too, thus defusing, although not dismissing, the atmosphere of foreboding created by the author's vivid opening description. The reader's identification with the heroine's discomfort and nervousness is brilliantly achieved by such seemingly insignificant details.

In the comfort of her flat we watch her go through the motions of one home after a long, hard day at work. Her feeling that she is not alone and that she is being watched is superbly captured, not least of all in the evocative description of the flash of movement *almost* caught out of the corner of her eye. We share her rising panic as the story builds to a chillingly original climax.

Critic 2

This is yet another of those nasty, prurient stories in which the reader is invited to join in a titillating masculinist fantasy of rape and domination. The scenario is familiar: a woman alone in her flat becomes increasingly terrified that someone is in her home watching her.

It's all done with great skill, of course. There's the "wild and stormy night" atmosphere, the references to a faintly malevolent physical setting, and the heroine is completely recognizable in that she is young, slightly built, attractive and, moreover, frequently naked. It's real peeping-Tom stuff, as cinematic stereotypes are invoked to position readers as voyeurs. Hence we have not just an unclothed body but a series of quick close-ups of erect nipples, wet breasts, belly and thigh presented in the familiar contexts of the bathroom scene and the dressing table mirror tableau. Predictably, there is also "the flight," affording yet another opportunity for titillating flashes of flesh through the heroine's parting robe. Constructed as an object of desire, she is to be observed rather than pitied.

Her disintegration into terror is all that one would expect. She answers the telephone call of her boyfriend, who is everything she is not. He is calm, rational and efficient—and presumably fully clothed, as we hear nothing of *his* bodily reactions.

The conclusion might suggest that she, in fact, is the rational one, but this interpretation is hardly possible, lost as it is in a final gasp of lascivious pleasure. It is, after all, just what we have been led to expect by stories of this kind, which take the terror of women as a subject for entertainment.

Critic 3

The fact is, as usual, the feminists haven't understood that it's meant to be a joke. Both the reader and the hapless boyfriend are the victims of the author's mordant sense of humor. What could be funnier than our slightly dim-witted heroine spooking herself so thoroughly that she is unable to stay alone in her flat? The boyfriend gets it right the first time: this isn't to be taken seriously!

While the reader has to admire how cleverly Tony Hunter sets the scene, he then piles on the suspense in a totally and deliberately conventional way. The alternation of periods of comfort and relaxation with moments of sheer terror for the girl builds inexorably to the point where, in a scene echoing every B grade movie ever made of this genre, she pleads on the telephone for help. I laughed out loud at the last line where the receiver is re-placed in a final, extravagant re-working of this enjoyably predictable genre. The author's intention is clear. Readers surely cannot take this story seriously in any way; from the opening paragraph it is obvious what is going to happen and it is in the very familiarity and predictability of the plot that so much of the skill of the author and the pleasure of the reading lie.

■ Write a paragraph briefly summarizing what you consider to be the main differences between the critics' readings.

How Are Such Different Readings Possible?

It seems that these critics are not only foregrounding and silencing different textual fragments or bits of the text to produce their readings. They also appear to be reading in different ways.

The first critic might be argued to be producing what has been called an *aesthetic* reading, which focuses on how "well" the author has written the story. The second critic could be said to be constructing a *gendered* reading, by drawing attention to issues of gender and possible power relationships supported by the text. The third critic, in asserting that it's all just a joke, appears to be claiming to produce a more reasonable or *objective* reading.

■ Below are listed some ways of trying to summarize features of different reading practices or ways of reading. With a partner, try to decide which of the suggested features could be applied or related to the critics' readings of "Listen to the End." For each way of reading, make a check mark for each critic you think reads the story in that way.

Features of Ways of Reading	Critic 1	Critic 2	Critic 3
Analyzing the style of writing			
Measuring the writer's skill in terms of a particular genre			
Finding proof of the author's "originality"			
Assessing the quality of the writing			
Foregrounding issues of gender			
Seeing stories as a reflection of life			
Emphasizing the formula features of the text			
Questioning the text and the values it supports			
Looking for a single theme or meaning in the text			
Seeing stories as structuring meanings by which a culture lives			
Looking for gaps, silences, and contradictions in texts and readings			
Seeing stories as entertainment			

Which Reading and Why?

Because it is no longer considered possible to argue that a reading is right or wrong on the basis of there being a fixed meaning in the text, it has been suggested that readers both construct readings and choose between or among them on the basis of shared values and beliefs.

■ With a partner, see if you can match each of the following descriptions to one of the three critic's readings you have just considered.

Description A

This reading questions the sexist values that dominant readings of the text appear to support. Analysis of the ways in which particular readings are produced and what they might support is assumed to be important. It is argued that meaning is located not in the text but in the ways in which gender is constructed. Reading is thought of in social and political ways.

Description B

This reading supports dominant power relationships between women and men by not questioning them. Instead, the important issues of reading a text are located in questions of aesthetics—that is, how well a text is written. This approach has the effect of marginalizing other readings by simply not acknowledging the possibility that they even exist.

Description C

This reading acknowledges the possibility of other readings, especially feminist ones, but challenges them by claiming a kind of distance or objectivity, which the critic claims is authorized by the text. That is, the critic argues that this is the correct way to read the text. This is an attempt to marginalize or silence readings of gender issues as humorless and misguided.

Of course, these "descriptions" are readings too—of the critics' readings! You could analyze the construction of these descriptions, and probably should do so, since there is no such thing as a neutral text or a neutral reading. Each of these descriptions, then, is a *reading* and can be argued to serve the interests of different groups of people.

■ Can you decide which of the earlier critics' readings are supported by this book?

Like *all* the books you read, this book is trying to *position* you to produce a particular reading. It argues that you should always ask how and why a text might be read in a particular way—and that includes this one. These issues are discussed further in the next chapters.

2 Readings and Reading Positions

To help you to analyze the construction of possible readings of two unconventional narrative texts in this chapter, you are asked to explore the idea of readings further and to consider the concept of *reading positions.*

It has been suggested that texts provide readers with reading positions from which the text can be read and understood. In other words, a text may offer a position to readers from which to produce a particular reading from a range of possible readings.

Readers, however, cannot be forced to accept a position or to produce the reading a text appears to invite. Readers can resist the position offered and construct *alternative* or *resistant* readings that support other values or beliefs.

Alternative or resistant readings of texts were once explained as being due to differences in readers' personal opinions. Individual readers were said to interpret texts in the light of their experiences.

Recent theory, however, argues that experience is not personal but cultural. That is, although you, as an individual, may have an experience—such as falling off a bike, loving someone, or winning a prize—you can only think about those experiences in particular ways that are available to you. So, it is argued, readers read texts and fill gaps not with ideas that they personally "make up," but with meanings that are *already available* in their culture.

The different ways readers can make meaning from texts—the range of reading positions they can take up—depends on their *access* to differing ideas in their culture. That is, it is possible to be a resistant reader of what has come to be the dominant reading of a text, if you have access to ways of thinking which challenge that reading.

"The Scarlatti Tilt"

The activities that follow this story are designed to:

- help you to analyze the construction of your reading;

- consider the idea of readings and "where they come from";
- explore the concept of reading positions;
- introduce you to the argument that texts are, in a sense, always "already read."

The Scarlatti Tilt

Richard Brautigan

"It's very hard to live in a studio apartment in San Jose with a man who's learning to play the violin."

That's what she told the police when she handed them the empty revolver.

Constructing a Reading

- "The Scarlatti Tilt" is a very short story. Reread it a few times and then, with a partner, construct as detailed a reading of it as you can, using the following questions as starting points. Make brief notes to help you describe your reading to others.

  a. What has happened?
  b. Why has it happened?
  c. What is the setting?
  d. What is it like?
  e. Who is involved?
  f. What are they like?

- With another pair, share notes and discuss the similarities and differences between your reading and theirs.
- In a class discussion, compare readings of the story produced by different pairs. Take note of similarities and differences that seem to have occurred. How would you explain these? Are there particular words or phrases of the text that might support or account for the production of certain readings?

Where Do the Readings Come From?

The questions above encouraged you to produce readings of the plot, setting, and characters. Although "The Scarlatti Tilt" is very short, readers usually are able to construct readings that are quite detailed.

Because readers find it so easy to produce readings of "The Scarlatti Tilt," the ways in which they operate to do it are often invisible. It seems, for example, that readers are not always able to account for their reading by making reference to "what's on the page." It seems almost easier to point to gaps than to bits of the text or textual fragments. There are, after all, only thirty-seven words (including the title) "on the page."

Constructing Readings

Readers can construct detailed readings of "The Scarlatti Tilt" because:

■ Debate, in your group, and then with your class, which of the following assertions might best explain how readers can produce detailed readings of "The Scarlatti Tilt."

1. The meaning is obvious from the story.
2. Readers read "between the lines."
3. Readers make logical inferences from the information given.
4. The story is like other stories of this kind which readers recognize.
5. Readers fill gaps with already available readings or sets of meanings.
6. There are readings of this type of text already available to readers.
7. Readers use imagination to make sense of the story.

Tilting the Tilt

"The Scarlatti Tilt" can be read as a tale of the killing of one human being by another. To claim, then, that this is a humorous text might seem odd. But this is a common, even usual, reading of the story.

■ Read the stories that follow. Keeping in mind your exploration of *how* readers might produce readings (see Chapter 1), comment, in a class discussion, on how readings might be changed by the alterations made below. You could begin by focusing on whether the altered text is more or less easily read as a humorous story and *why*.

The Scarlatti Tilt (Alternate A)
"It's very hard to live in a studio apartment in San Jose with a woman who's learning to play the violin." That's what he told the police when he handed them the empty revolver.

The Scarlatti Tilt (Alternate B)
"It's very hard to live in a studio apartment in San Jose with a child who's learning to play the violin." That's what she told the police when she handed them the empty revolver.

The Scarlatti Tilt (Alternate C)
"It's very hard to live in a studio apartment in San Jose with a baby who cries all the time." That's what he told the police when he handed them the empty revolver.

The Scarlatti Tilt (Alternate D)
"It's very hard to live in a studio apartment in San Jose with a baby who cries all the time." That's what she told the police when she handed them the empty revolver.

The Pacific Tilt? (Alternate E)
"It's very hard to live in a beach house in Monterey with a man who's learning to surf." That's what she told the police when she handed them the empty harpoon.

The "Already Read"

One possible reason for the changes that seem to occur when a text is altered, is that there are already-available readings or ways of thinking about issues that are *activated* by particular texts.

For example, the linking of violence with women and children now appears to produce a reading that is not humorous. This has not always been so. References to "beating the wife" and to women and children needing regular beltings might have been widely viewed as "just a joke" some years ago. However, there is now a powerful reading of the connection between violence and women and children as unacceptable and certainly not a laughing matter.

"The Scarlatti Tilt," however, is often read as humorous. Does this mean that the connection between violence and men *is* acceptable? While it is possible to say "Of course it isn't!" there are ways in which violence (perhaps called something else) is ambiguously part of the construction of masculinity.

Is it, perhaps, the fact that men as a "category" are not usually read as victims of violence (although clearly they often are) that allows for a humorous response? If they are read as powerful, then laughter can seem largely acceptable. This is changed, however, if particular groups of men—those who are often targets of violence—are named. This may result in particular groups of readers either producing racist or homophobic readings, or, alternatively, objecting to such readings as offensive and unacceptable.

In reading an apparently simple little story, such as "The Scarlatti Tilt," readers could be argued to be producing—or reproducing—readings of gender and violence and humor that are already available to them in their culture and society at a particular time.

- In your group, talk about the issues raised by your reading of the passage above, and then discuss them as a class.

"How I Contemplated . . ."

The following story by Joyce Carol Oates has a title and subtitle longer than all of "The Scarlatti Tilt":

> **How I Contemplated the World from the Detroit House of Correction and Began My Life Over Again**
>
> *Notes for an Essay for an English Class at Baldwin Country Day School; Poking around in Debris; Disgust and Curiosity; A Revelation of the Meaning of Life; A Happy Ending . . .*

Fragments

The story that follows the title is over 5,500 words long. Yet it is still, like all texts, a fragmentary text with contradictions and gaps. The text, in fact, draws attention to its incompleteness by claiming to be "Notes for an Essay." There is a series of sub-headings, under which appear apparent jottings for an essay to be written for an "English Class at Baldwin Country Day School." And yet the "notes" are published in a short story anthology—which suggests to readers that this text is to be read in certain ways.

The following activity asks you to read a short text in two different ways, and then to consider:

- the differences in the readings you produce;
- how you operate as a reader to produce different readings.

Reading Notes

- Read the following lines as a list or series of notes and, with a partner, suggest what they could be notes for:

  School shots? Exclusive—school hall? formal gardens?
  Sound? Period, '67? Music?
  Locations?—white wealthy neighborhood; city/downtown mean streets.
  Other? department store—upscale;
  paneled library—private; squat—squalid—decaying tenement?
  detention center—women's; doctor's surgery/clinic?
  Sleazy? Upscale? Both?
  girl, white, long brown hair, innocent looking;
  woman, white, late 20s?, 30s? streetwise;
  man, blonde curls, decadent, worn 30s;
  drug pushers, prostitutes; police;
  inmates of women's detention center—black, white;
  hospital—public & private?
  mother—well-preserved, expensive—late 30s, early 40s?
  father—doctor, lucrative private practice; cars?

Reading Narrative

- Now, reread the same lines as a short narrative. This might mean making connections between items, filling gaps, combining events in certain ways, and making assumptions about the characters.
- Divide your note page into two columns headed, respectively, "Notes" and "Narrative." With a partner, list points to show how you operate differently as a reader to produce a reading of the lines as notes or as narrative.

- In your group, compare lists. Then make suggestions about the type of story you consider the lines could be read as referring to.
- In a class discussion, list suggestions made regarding (a) the possible differences in reading practices or ways of reading you have discussed, and (b) the type of story you would regard as likely to be constructed from such lines. Try to explain the occurrence of any marked similarities or differences in the suggested stories.

Why Can It Seem Difficult to Read?

Joyce Carol Oates's story "How I Contemplated . . ." can seem difficult to read because it challenges many assumptions of what a story should be like. It looks different, for a start, with numbered sections and subheadings appearing intermittently throughout.

The text also disrupts many expectations of how plots are constructed by shifting time and place frequently. And the characters are introduced in sections that appear to be trying to convince the reader that they are notes. For example, a character is referred to as "twenty, twenty-five, she is thirty or more?" Read as notes, these words could indicate a decision still to be made by the writer; however, if the text is assumed to be part of a narrative, then it could be read as a sign that the character's age is hard to judge.

Readers and writers share assumptions about what notes and stories are like, although it's hard to pin down exactly the differences between the two types of text. The difficulty here appears to lie in the disruption of reading positions. That is, it is hard to recognize what type of text "How I Contemplated . . ." might be, and, in turn, hard to work out a way of reading it. The following activities, therefore, are designed to help you produce a reading of the story before you read it!

Following is an extract from "How I Contemplated. . . ." Apparently in note form, the extract can be read as part of a narrative, and it is possible to construct quite detailed readings of "Sioux Drive" in terms of class, race, and gender, as well as readings of the "speaker" and her position in relation to what is listed.

- In your group, produce a reading of the neighborhood, the speaker, and the type of story you think the extract might be from.

V. Sioux Drive

George, Clyde G. 240 Sioux. A manufacturer's representative; children, a dog, a wife. Georgian with the usual columns. You think of the White House, then of Thomas Jefferson, then your mind goes blank on the white pillars and you think of nothing. Norris, Ralph W. 246 Sioux. Public relations. Colonial. Bay window, brick, stone, concrete, green shutters, sidewalk, lantern, grass, trees, black-top drive, two children, one of them my classmate Esther (Esther Norris) at Baldwin. Wife, cars. Ramsey, Michael D. 250 Sioux. Colonial. Big living room, thirty by twenty five, fireplaces in living room, library, recreation room, panelled walls wet bar five bathrooms five bedrooms two lavatories central air conditioning automatic sprinkler garage door three children one wife two cars a breakfast room a patio a large fenced lot fourteen trees a front door with a brass knocker never knocked. Next is our house. Classic contemporary. Traditional modern. Attached garage, attached Florida room, attached patio, attached pool and cabana, attached roof. A front door mail slot through which pour *Time Magazine, Fortune, Life, Business Week, The Wall Street Journal, The New York Times, The New Yorker, The Saturday Review, M.D., Modern Medicine, Disease of the Month;* and also . . . And in addition to this, a quiet sealed letter from Baldwin saying: Your daughter is not doing work compatible with her performance on the Stanford-Binet [an intelligence test].

Notes for a Plot?

The list below could also be "notes." The items might be read as having no connection at all. "She" could refer to a number of different girls or women. The events could be read as totally unrelated.

If you read them as constituting a narrative, however, you may be aware of being able to draw on available readings of (a) the types of events listed, (b) how you might sequence them, (c) the types of characters who might be involved, and (d) the type of story you might produce.

■ Share the task, with a partner, of copying the following notes onto separate pieces of paper. Then, sequence them to produce a story.

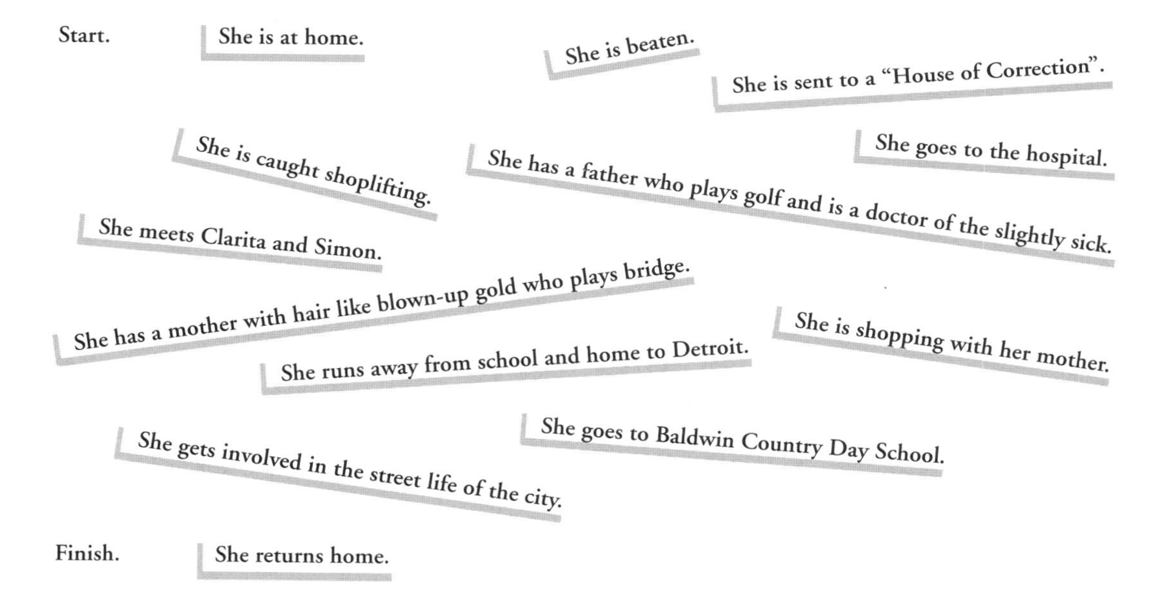

■ Now share some of the resulting stories in a class discussion before reading the text of "How I Contemplated . . . ," which follows.

How I Contemplated the World from the Detroit House of Correction and Began My Life Over Again

Notes for an Essay for an English Class at Baldwin Country Day School; Poking Around in Debris; Disgust and Curiosity; A Revelation of the Meaning of Life; A Happy Ending . . .

Joyce Carol Oates

I. Events

1. The girl (myself) is walking through Branden's, that excellent store. Suburb of a large famous city that is a symbol for large famous American cities. The event sneaks up on the girl, who believes she is herding it along with a small fixed smile, a girl of fifteen, innocently experienced. She dawdles in a certain style by a counter of costume jewelry. Rings, earrings, necklaces. Prices from $5 to $50, all within reach. All ugly. She eases over to the glove counter, where everything is ugly too. In her close-fitted coat with its black fur collar she contemplates the luxury of Branden's, which she has known for many years: its many mild pale lights, easy on the eye and the soul, its elaborate tinkly decorations, its women shoppers with their excellent shoes and coats and hairdos, all dawdling gracefully, in no hurry.

Who was ever in a hurry here?

2. The girl seated at home. A small library, panelled walls of oak. Someone is talking to me. An earnest, husky, female voice drives itself against my ears, nervous, frightened, groping around my heart, saying, "If you wanted gloves, why didn't you say so? Why didn't you ask for them?" That store, Branden's, is owned by Raymond Forrest who lives on Du Maurier Drive. We live on Sioux Drive. Raymond Forrest. A handsome man? An ugly man? A man of fifty or sixty, with gray hair, or a man of forty with earnest, courteous eyes, a good golf game; who is Raymond Forrest, this man who is my salvation? Father has been talking to him. Father is not his physician; Dr. Berg is his physician. Father and Dr. Berg refer patients to each other. There is a connection. Mother plays bridge with . . . On Mondays and Wednesdays our maid Billie works at . . . The strings draw together in a cat's cradle, making a net to save you when you fall . . .

3. Harriet Arnold's. A small shop, better than Branden's. Mother in her black coat, I in my close-fitted blue coat. Shopping. Now look at this, isn't this cute, do you want this, why don't you want this, try this on, take this with you to the fitting room, take this also, what's wrong with you, what can I do for you, why are you so strange . . . ? "I wanted to steal but not to buy," I don't tell her. The girl droops along in her coat and gloves and leather boots, her eyes scan the horizon, which is pastel pink and decorated like Branden's, tasteful walls and modern ceilings with graceful glimmering lights.

4. Weeks later, the girl at a bus stop. Two o'clock in the afternoon, a Tuesday; obviously she has walked out of school.

5. The girl stepping down from a bus. Afternoon, weather changing to colder. Detroit. Pavement and closed-up stores; grillwork over the windows of a pawnshop. What is a pawnshop, exactly?

II. Characters

1. The girl stands five feet five inches tall. An ordinary height. Baldwin Country Day School draws them up to that height. She dreams along the corridors and presses her face against the Thermoplex glass. No frost or steam can ever form on that glass. A smudge of grease from her forehead . . . could she be boiled down to grease? She wears her hair loose and long and straight in suburban teen-age style, 1968. Eyes smudged with pencil, dark brown. Brown hair. Vague green eyes. A pretty girl? An ugly girl? She sings to herself under her breath, idling in the corridor, thinking of her many secrets (the thirty dollars she once took from the purse of a friend's mother, just for fun, the basement window she smashed in her own house just for fun) and thinking of her brother who is at Susquehanna Boys' Academy, an excellent preparatory school in Maine, remembering him unclearly . . . he has long manic hair and a squeaking voice and he looks like one of the popular teen-age singers of 1968, one of those in a group, The Certain Forces, The Way Out, The Maniacs Responsible. The girl in her turn looks like one of those fieldsful of girls who listen to the boys' singing, dreaming and mooning restlessly, breaking into high sullen laughter, innocently experienced.

2. The mother. A Midwestern woman of Detroit and suburbs. Belongs to the Detroit Athletic Club. Also the Detroit Golf Club. Also the Bloomfield Hills Country Club. The Village Women's Club at which lectures are given each winter on Genet and Sartre and James Baldwin,[1] by the Director of the Adult Education Program at Wayne State University . . . The Bloomfield Art Association. Also the Founders Society of the Detroit Institute of Arts. Also . . . Oh, she is in perpetual motion, this lady, hair like blown-up gold and finer than gold, hair and fingers and body of inestimable grace. Heavy weighs the gold on the back of her hairbrush and hand mirror. Heavy heavy the candlesticks in the dining room. Very heavy is the big car, a Lincoln, long and black, that on one cool autumn day split a squirrel's body in two unequal parts.

3. The father. Dr. _______. He belongs to the same clubs as #2. A player of squash and golf; he has a golfer's umbrella of stripes. Candy stripes. In his mouth nothing turns to sugar, however; saliva works no miracles here. His doctoring is of the slightly sick. The sick are sent elsewhere (to Dr. Berg?), the deathly sick are sent back for more tests and their bills are sent to their homes, the unsick are sent to Dr. Coronet (Isabel, a lady), an excellent psychiatrist for unsick people who angrily believe they are sick and want to do something about it. If they demand a male psychiatrist, the unsick are sent by Dr. _______ (my father) to Dr. Lowenstein, a male psychiatrist, excellent and expensive, with a limited practice.

1. Jean Genet (1910–86), French novelist and playwright; Jean Paul Sartre (1905–80), French novelist, dramatist, and philosopher; James Baldwin (1924–87), American novelist and essayist.

4. Clarita. She is twenty, twenty-five, she is thirty or more? Pretty, ugly, what? She is a woman lounging by the side of a road, in jeans and a sweater, hitchhiking, or she is slouched on a stool at a counter in some roadside diner. A hard line of jaw. Curious eyes. Amused eyes. Behind her eyes processions move, funeral pageants, cartoons. She says, "I never can figure out why girls like you bum around down here. What are you looking for anyway?" An odour of tobacco about her. Unwashed underclothes, or no underclothes, unwashed skin, gritty toes, hair long and falling into strands, not recently washed.

5. Simon. In this city the weather changes abruptly, so Simon's weather changes abruptly. He sleeps through the afternoon. He sleeps through the morning. Rising, he gropes around for something to get him going, for a cigarette or a pill to drive him out to the street where the temperature is hovering around 35°. Why doesn't it drop? Why, why doesn't the cold clean air come down from Canada; will he have to go up to Canada to get it? Will he have to leave the Country of his Birth and sink into Canada's frosty fields . . . ? Will the F.B.I. (which he dreams about constantly) chase him over the Canadian border on foot, hounded out in a blizzard of broken glass and horns . . . ?

"Once I was Huckleberry Finn," Simon says, "But now I am Roderick Usher."[2] Beset by frenzies and fears, this man who makes my spine go cold, he takes green pills, yellow pills, pills of white and capsules of dark blue and green . . . he takes other things I may not mention, for what if Simon seeks me out and climbs into my girl's bedroom here in Bloomfield Hills and strangles me, what then . . . ? (As I write this I begin to shiver. Why do I shiver? I am now sixteen and sixteen is not an age for shivering.) It comes from Simon, who is always cold.

III. World Events
Nothing.

IV. People and Circumstances Contributing to This Delinquency
Nothing.

V. Sioux Drive
George, Clyde G. 240 Sioux. A manufacturer's representative; children, a dog, a wife. Georgian with the usual columns. You think of the White House, then of Thomas Jefferson, then your mind goes blank on the white pillars and you think of nothing. Norris, Ralph W. 246 Sioux. Public relations. Colonial. Bay window, brick, stone, concrete, wood, green shutters, sidewalk, lantern, grass, trees, black-top drive, two children, one of them my classmate Esther (Esther Norris) at Baldwin. Wife, cars. Ramsey, Michael D. 250 Sioux. Colonial. Big living room, thirty by twenty-five, fireplaces in living room, library, recreation room, panelled walls wet bar five bathrooms five bedrooms two lavatories central air conditioning automatic sprinkler automatic garage door three children one wife two cars a breakfast room a patio a large fenced lot fourteen trees a front door with a brass knocker never knocked. Next is our house. Classic contemporary. Traditional modern. Attached garage, attached Florida room,

2. i.e. he has changed from a wholesome American boy into a morbid neurotic. Usher is the chief character in Edgar Alan Poe's *Fall of the House of Usher.* Huck Finn is the young hero of Mark Twain's novel *The Adventures of Huckleberry Finn.*

attached patio, attached pool and cabana, attached roof. A front door mail slot through which pour *Time Magazine, Fortune, Life, Business Week, The Wall Street Journal, The New York Times, The New Yorker, The Saturday Review, M.D., Modern Medicine, Disease of the Month* . . . and also . . . And in addition to all this, a quiet sealed letter from Baldwin saying: Your daughter is not doing work compatible with her performance on the Stanford-Binet[3] . . . And your son is not doing well, not well at all, very sad. Where is your son anyway? Once he stole trick-and-treat candy from some six-year-old kids, he himself being a robust ten. The beginning. Now your daughter steals. In the Village Pharmacy she made off with, yes she did, don't deny it, she made off with a copy of *Pageant Magazine* for no reason, she swiped a roll of Life Savers in a green wrapper and was in no need of saving her life or even in need of sucking candy; when she was no more than eight years old she stole, don't blush, she stole a package of Tums only because it was out on the counter and available, and the nice lady behind the counter (now dead) said nothing. . . . Sioux Drive. Maples, oaks, elms. Diseased elms cut down. Sioux Drive runs into Roosevelt Drive. Slow, turning lanes, not streets, all drives and lanes and ways and passes. A private police force. Quiet private police, in unmarked cars. Cruising on Saturday evenings with paternal smiles for the residents who are streaming in and out of houses, going to and from parties, a thousand parties, slightly staggering, the women in their furs alighting from automobiles bought of Ford and General Motors and Chrysler, very heavy automobiles. No foreign cars. Detroit. In 275 Sioux, down the block in that magnificent French-Normandy mansion, lives __________ himself, who has the C_____________ account itself, imagine that! Look at where he lives and look at the enormous trees and chimneys, imagine his many fireplaces, imagine his wife and children, imagine his wife's hair, imagine her fingernails, imagine her bathtub of smooth clean glowing pink, imagine their embraces, his trouser pockets filled with odd coins and keys and dust and peanuts, imagine their ecstasy on Sioux Drive, imagine their income tax returns, imagine their little boy's pride in his experimental car, a scaled down C_____________, as he roars round the neighbourhood on the sidewalks frightening dogs and Negro maids, oh imagine all these things, imagine everything, let your mind roar out all over Sioux Drive and Du Maurier Drive and Roosevelt Drive and Ticonderoga Pass and Burning Bush Way and Lincolnshire Pass and Lois Lane.

When spring comes, its winds blow nothing to Sioux Drive, no odours of hollyhocks or forsythia, nothing Sioux Drive doesn't already possess, everything is planted and performing. The weather vanes, had they weather vanes, don't have to turn with the wind, don't have to contend with the weather. There is no weather.

VI. Detroit

There is always weather in Detroit. Detroit's temperature is always 32°. Fast-falling temperatures. Slow-rising temperatures. Wind from the north-northeast four to forty miles an hour, small-craft warnings, partly cloudy today and Wednesday changing to partly sunny through Thursday . . . small warnings of frost, soot warnings, traffic warnings, hazardous lake conditions for small craft and swimmers, restless Negro gangs,

3. An intelligence test.

restless cloud formations, restless temperatures aching to fall out the very bottom of the thermometer or shoot up over the top and boil everything over in red mercury.

Detroit's temperature is 32°. Fast-falling temperatures. Slow-rising temperatures. Wind from the north-northeast four to forty miles an hour . . .

VII. Events

1. The girl's heart is pounding. In her pocket is a pair of gloves! In a plastic bag! Airproof breathproof plastic bag, gloves selling for twenty-five dollars on Branden's counter! In her pocket! Shoplifted! . . . In her purse is a blue comb, not very clean. In her purse is a leather billfold (a birthday present from her grandmother in Philadelphia) with snapshots of the family in clean plastic windows, in the billfold are bills, she does't know how many bills . . . In her purse is an ominous note from her friend Tykie What's this about Joe H. and the kids hanging around at Louise's Sat. night? You heard anything? . . . passed in French class. In her purse is a lot of dirty yellow Kleenex, her mother's heart would break to see such very dirty Kleenex, and at the bottom of her purse are brown hairpins and safety pins and a broken pencil and a ballpoint pen (blue) stolen from somewhere forgotten and a purse-size compact of Cover Girl Make-Up, Ivory Rose . . . Her lipstick is Broken Heart, a corrupt pink; her fingers are trembling like crazy; her teeth are beginning to chatter; her insides are alive; her eyes glow in her head; she is saying to her mother's astonished face I want to steal but not to buy.

2. At Clarita's. Day or night? What room is this? A bed, a regular bed, and a mattress on the floor nearby. Wallpaper hanging in strips. Clarita says she tore it like that with her teeth. She was fighting a barbaric tribe that night, high from some pills; she was battling for her life with men wearing helmets of heavy iron and their faces no more than Christian crosses to breathe through, every one of those bastards looking like her lover Simon, who seems to breathe with great difficulty through the slits of mouth and nostrils in his face. Clarita has never heard of Sioux Drive. Raymond Forrest cuts no ice with her, nor does the C_____________ account and its millions; Harvard Business School could be at the corner of Vernor and 12th Street for all she cares, and Vietnam might have sunk by now into the Dead Sea under its tons of debris, for all the amazement she could show . . . her face is overworked, overwrought, at the age of twenty (thirty?) it is already exhausted but fanciful and ready for a laugh. Clarita says mournfully to me Honey somebody is going to turn you out let me give you warning. In a movie shown on late television Clarita is not a mess like this but a nurse, with short neat hair and a dedicated look, in love with her doctor and her doctor's patients and their diseases, enamoured of needles and sponges and rubbing alcohol. . . . Or no: she is a private secretary. Robert Cummings is her boss. She helps him with fantastic plots, the canned audience laughs, no, the audience doesn't laugh because nothing is funny, instead her boss is Robert Taylor and they are not boss and secretary but husband and wife, she is threatened by a young starlet, she is grim, handsome, wifely, a good companion for a good man . . . She is Claudette Colbert. Her sister too is Claudette Colbert. They are twins, identical. Her husband Charles Boyer[4] is a very rich handsome man and her sister, Claudette Colbert, is plotting her death in order to take her place as

4. Boyer, Colbert, Taylor, and Cummings are romantic film stars of the 1940s and '50s.

the rich man's wife, no one will know because they are twins. All these marvellous lives Clarita might have lived, but she fell out the bottom at the age of thirteen. At the age when I was packing my overnight case for a slumber party at Toni Deshield's she was tearing filthy sheets off a bed and scratching up a rash on her arms . . . Thirteen is uncommonly young for a white girl in Detroit, Miss Brock of the Detroit House of Correction said in a sad newspaper interview for the Detroit News; fifteen and sixteen are more likely. What can we do? Taxes are rising and the tax base is falling. The temperature rises slowly but falls rapidly. Everything is falling out the bottom, Woodward Avenue is filthy, Livernois Avenue is filthy! Scraps of paper flutter in the air like pigeons, dirt flies up and hits you right in the eye, oh Detroit is breaking up into dangerous bits of newspaper and dirt, watch out . . .

Clarita's apartment is over a restaurant. Simon her lover emerges from the cracks at dark. Mrs. Olesko, a neighbor of Clarita's, an aged white wisp of a woman, doesn't complain but sniffs with contentment at Clarita's noisy life and doesn't tell the cops, hating cops, when the cops arrive. I should give more fake names, more blanks, instead of telling all these secrets. I myself am a secret; I am a minor.

3. My father reads a paper at a medical convention in Los Angeles. There he is, on the edge of the North American continent, when the unmarked detective put his hand so gently on my arm in the aisle of Branden's and said, "Miss, would you like to step over here for a minute?"

And where was he when Clarita put her hand on my arm, that wintry dark sulphurous aching day in Detroit, in the company of closed-down barber shops, closed-down diners, closed-down movie houses, homes, windows, basements, faces . . . she put her hand on my arm and said, "Honey, are you looking for somebody down here?"

And was he home worrying about me, gone for two weeks solid, when they carried me off . . .? It took three of them to get me in the police cruiser, so they said, and they put more than their hands on my arm.

4. I work on this lesson. My English teacher is Mr. Forest, who is from Michigan State. Not handsome, Mr. Forest, and his name is plain, unlike Raymond Forrest's, but he is sweet and rodentlike, he has conferred with the principal and my parents, and everything is fixed . . . treat her as if nothing has happened, a new start, begin again, only sixteen years old, what a shame, how did it happen?—nothing happened, nothing could have happened, a slight physiological modification known only to a gynecologist or to Dr. Coronet. I work on my lesson. I sit in my pink room. I look around the room with my sad pink eyes. I sigh. I dawdle, I pause. I eat up time. I am limp and happy to be home, I am sixteen years old suddenly, my head hangs heavy as a pumpkin on my shoulders, and my hair has just been cut by Mr. Faye at the Crystal Salon and is said to be very becoming.

(Simon too put his hand on my arm and said, "Honey, you have got to come with me," and in his six-by-six room we got to know each other. Would I go back to Simon again? Would I lie down with him in all that filth and craziness? Over and over again.

a Clarita is being betrayed as in front of a Cunningham Drug Store she is nervously eyeing a coloured man who may or may not have money, or a nervous white boy of twenty with sideburns and an Appalachian look, who may or may not have a knife hidden in his jacket pocket, or a husky red-faced man of friendly countenance who may or may not be a member of the Vice Squad out for an early twilight walk.)

I work on my lesson for Mr. Forest. I have filled up eleven pages. Words pour out of me and won't stop. I want to tell everything . . . Simon's friend in a very new trench coat with an old high school graduation ring on his finger . . .? Simon's bearded friend? When I was down too low for him, Simon kicked me out and gave me to him for three days, I think, on Fourteenth Street in Detroit, an airy room of cold cruel drafts with newspapers on the floor. Do I really remember that or am I piecing it together from what they told me? Did they tell the truth? Did they know much of the truth?

VIII. Characters

1. Wednesdays after school, at four; Saturday mornings at ten. Mother drives me to Dr. Coronet. Ferns in the office, plastic or real, they look the same. Dr. Coronet is queenly, an elegant nicotine-stained lady who would have studied with Freud had circumstances not prevented it, a bit of a Catholic, ready to offer you some mystery if your teeth will ache too much without it. Highly recommended by Father! Forty dollars an hour, Father's forty dollars! Progress! Looking up! Looking better! That new haircut is so becoming, says Dr. Coronet herself, showing how normal she is for a woman with an I.Q. of 180 and many advanced degrees.

2. Mother. A lady in a brown suede coat. Boots of shiny black material, black gloves, a black fur hat. She would be humiliated could she know that of all the people in the world it is my ex-lover Simon who walks most like her . . . self-conscious and unreal, listening to distant music, a little bowlegged with craftiness . . .

3. Father. Tying a necktie. In a hurry. On my first evening home he put his hand on my arm and said, "Honey, we're going to forget all about this."

4. Simon. Outside, a plane is crossing the sky, in here we're in a hurry. Morning. It must be morning. The girl is half out of her mind, whimpering and vague; Simon her dear friend is wretched this morning . . . he is wretched with morning itself . . . he forces her to give him an injection with that needle she knows is filthy, she has a dread of needles and surgical instruments and the odour of things that are to be sent into the blood, thinking somehow of her father . . . This is a bad morning, Simon says that his mind is being twisted out of shape, and so he submits to the needle that he usually scorns and bites his lip with his yellowish teeth, his face going very pale. Ah baby! he says in his soft mocking voice, which with all women is a mockery of love, do it like this—Slowly—And the girl, terrified, almost drops the precious needle but manages to turn it up to the light from the window . . . is it an extension of herself then? She can give him this gift then? I wish you wouldn't do this to me, she says, wise in her terror, because it seems to her that Simon's danger—in a few minutes he may be dead—is a way of pressing her against him that is more powerful than any other embrace. She has to work over his arm, the knotted corded veins of his arm, her forehead wet with perspiration as she pushes and releases the needle, staring at that mixture of liquid now stained with Simon's bright blood . . . When the drug hits him she can feel it herself, she feels that magic that is more than any woman can give him, striking the back of his

head and making his face stretch as if with the impact of a terrible sun. She tries to embrace him but he pushes her aside and stumbles to his feet. Jesus Christ, he says . . .

5. Princess, a Negro girl of eighteen. What is her charge? She is closed-mouthed about it, shrewd and silent, you know that no one had to wrestle her to the sidewalk to get her in here; she came with dignity. In the recreation room she sits reading *Nancy Drew and the Jewel Box Mystery,* which inspires in her face tiny wrinkles of alarm and interest: what a face! Light brown skin, heavy shaded eyes, heavy eyelashes, a serious sinister dark brow, graceful fingers, graceful wristbones, graceful legs, lips, tongue, a sugar-sweet voice, a leggy stride more masculine than Simon's and my mother's, decked out in a dirty blouse and dirty white slacks; vaguely nautical is Princess' style . . . At breakfast she is in charge of clearing the table and leans over me, saying, Honey you sure you ate enough?

6. The girl lies sleeping, wondering. Why here, why not there? Why Bloomfield Hills and not jail? Why jail and not her pink room? Why downtown Detroit and not Sioux Drive? What is the difference? Is Simon all the difference? The girl's head is a parade of wonders. She is nearly sixteen, her breath is marvellous with wonders, not long ago she was colouring with crayons and now she is smearing the landscape with paints that won't come off and won't come off her fingers either. She says to the matron I am not talking about anything, not because everyone has warned her not to talk but because, because she will not talk; because she won't say anything about Simon, who is her secret. And she says to the matron, I won't go home, up until that night in the lavatory when everything was changed . . . "No, I won't go home I want to stay here," she says, listening to her own words with amazement, thinking that weeds might climb everywhere over that marvellous $180,000 house and dinosaurs might return to muddy the beige carpeting, but never, never will she reconcile four o'clock in the morning in Detroit with eight o'clock breakfasts in Bloomfield Hills . . . oh, she aches still for Simon's hands and his caressing breath, though he gave her little pleasure, he took everything from her (five-dollar bills, ten-dollar bills, passed into her numb hands by men and taken out of her hands by Simon) until she herself was passed into the hands of other men, police, when Simon evidently got tired of her and her hysteria . . . No, I won't go home, I don't want to be bailed out. The girl thinks as a Stubborn and Wayward Child (one of several charges lodged against her), and the matron understands her crazy white-rimmed eyes that are seeking out some new violence that will keep her in jail, should someone threaten to let her out. Such children try to strangle the matrons, the attendants, or one another . . . they want the locks locked forever, the doors nailed shut . . . and this girl is no different up until that night her mind is changed for her . . .

IX. That Night

Princess and Dolly, a little white girl of maybe fifteen, hardy however as a sergeant and in the House of Correction for armed robbery, corner her in the lavatory at the farthest sink and the other girls look away and file out to bed, leaving her. God, how she is beaten up! Why is she beaten up? Why do they pound her, why such hatred? Princess vents all the hatred of a thousand silent Detroit winters on her body, this girl whose body belongs to me, fiercely she rides across the Midwestern plains on this girl's tender bruised body . . . revenge on the oppressed minorities of America! revenge on the slaughtered Indians! revenge on the female sex, on the male sex, revenge on Bloomfield Hills, revenge revenge . . .

X. Detroit
In Detroit, weather weighs heavily upon everyone. The sky looms large. The horizon shimmers in smoke. Downtown the buildings are imprecise in the haze. Perpetual haze. Perpetual motion inside the haze. Across the choppy river is the city of Windsor, in Canada. Part of the continent has bunched up here and is bulging outward, at the tip of Detroit; a cold hard rain is forever falling on the expressways . . . Shoppers shop grimly, their cars are not parked in safe places, their windshields may be smashed and graceful ebony hands may drag them out through their shatterproof smashed windshields, crying, Revenge for the Indians! Ah, they all fear leaving Hudson's and being dragged to the very tip of the city and thrown off the parking roof of Cobo Hall, that expensive tomb, into the river . . .

XI. Characters We Are Forever Entwined With
1. Simon drew me into his tender rotting arms and breathed gravity into me. Then I came to earth, weighed down. He said, You are such a little girl, and he weighed me down with his delight. In the palms of his hands were teeth marks from his previous life experiences. He was thirty-five, they said. Imagine Simon in this room, in my pink room: he is about six feet tall and stoops slightly, in a feline cautious way, always thinking, always on guard, with his scuffed light suede shoes and his clothes that are anyone's clothes, slightly rumpled ordinary clothes that ordinary men might wear to not-bad jobs. Simon has fair long hair, curly hair, spent languid curls that are like . . . exactly like the curls of wood shavings to the touch, I am trying to be exact . . . and he smells of unheated mornings and coffee and too many pills coating his tongue with a faint green-white scum . . . Dear Simon, who would be panicked in this room and in this house (right now Billie is vacuuming next door in my parents' room; a vacuum cleaner's roar is a sign of all good things), Simon who is said to have come from a home not much different from this, years ago, fleeing all the carpeting and the polished banisters . . . Simon has a deathly face, only desperate people fall in love with it. His face is bony and cautious, the bones of his cheeks prominent as if with the rigidity of his ceaseless thinking, plotting, for he has to make money out of girls to whom money means nothing, they're so far gone they can hardly count it, and in a sense money means nothing to him either except as a way of keeping on with his life. Each Day's Proud Struggle, the title of a novel we could read at jail . . . Each day he needs a certain amount of money. He devours it. It wasn't love he uncoiled in me with his hollowed-out eyes and his courteous smile, that remnant of a prosperous past, but a dark terror that needed to press itself flat against him, or against another man . . . but he was the first, he came over to me and took my arm, a claim. We struggled on the stairs and I said, Let me loose, you're hurting my neck, my face, it was such a surprise that my skin hurt where he rubbed it, and afterwards we lay face to face and he breathed everything into me. In the end I think he turned me in.

2. Raymond Forrest. I just read this morning that Raymond Forrest's father, the chairman of the board at ___________, died of a heart attack on a plane bound for London. I would like to write Raymond Forrest a note of sympathy. I would like to

thank him for not pressing charges against me one hundred years ago, saving me, being so generous . . . well, men like Raymond Forrest are generous men, not like Simon. I would like to write him a letter telling of my love, or of some other emotion that is positive and healthy. Not like Simon and his poetry, which he scrawled down when he was high and never changed a word . . . but when I try to think of something to say, it is Simon's language that comes back to me, caught in my head like a bad song, it is always Simon's language:

There is no reality only dreams
Your neck may get snapped when you wake
My love is drawn to some violent end
She keeps wanting to get away
My love is heading downward
And I am heading upward
She is going to crash on the sidewalk
And I am going to dissolve into the clouds

XII. Events

1. Out of the hospital, bruised and saddened and converted, with Princess' grunts still tangled in my hair . . . and Father in his overcoat, looking like a prince himself, come to carry me off. Up the expressway and out north to home. Jesus Christ, but the air is thinner and cleaner here. Monumental houses. Heartbreaking side-walks, so clean.

2. Weeping in the living room. The ceiling is two storeys high and two chandeliers hang from it. Weeping, weeping, though Billie the maid is probably listening. I will never leave home again. Never. Never leave home. Never leave this home again, never.

3. Sugar doughnuts for breakfast. The toaster is very shiny and my face is distorted in it. Is that my face?

4. The car is turning in the driveway. Father brings me home. Mother embraces me. Sunlight breaks in movieland patches on the roof of our traditional-contemporary home, which was designed for the famous automotive stylist whose identity, if I told you the name of the famous car he designed, you would all know, so I can't tell you because my teeth chatter at the thought of being sued . . . or having someone climb into my bedroom window with a rope to strangle me . . . The car turns up the blacktop drive. The house opens to me like a doll's house, so lovely in the sunlight, the big living room beckons to me with its walls falling away in a delirium of joy at my return, Billie the maid is no doubt listening from the kitchen as I burst into tears and the hysteria Simon got so sick of. Convulsed in Father's arms, I say I will never leave again, never, why did I leave, where did I go, what happened, my mind is gone wrong, my body is one big bruise, my backbone was sucked dry, it wasn't the men who hurt me and Simon never hurt me but only those girls . . . my God, how they hurt me . . . I will never leave home again . . . The car is perpetually turning up the drive and I am perpetually breaking down in the living room and we are perpetually taking the right exit from the expressway (Lahser Road) and the wall of the rest room is perpetually banging against my head and perpetually are Simon's hands moving across my body and adding everything up and so too are Father's hands on my shaking bruised back, far from the surface of my skin on the surface of my good blue cashmere coat (dry-cleaned for my

release) . . . I weep for all the money here, for God in gold and beige carpeting, for the beauty of chandeliers and the miracle of a clean polished gleaming toaster and faucets that run both hot and cold water, and I tell them, I will never leave home, this is my home, I love everything here, I am in love with everything here . . .

I am home.

Constructing a Reading

The romance, the western, comedy, science fiction, and fantasy are all familiar types of narratives, or *genres.* Each names a type of narrative which can be read as organizing events and characters according to repeated and therefore familiar conventions of story. Such conventions help readers "recognize" the kind of readings they might produce.

Many readers find "How I Contemplated . . ." initially difficult, perhaps because connections between this text and others, which seem more conventionally constructed, do not seem obvious. The text does not seem to belong to a familiar genre, and so readers may have trouble in knowing "how to read" it.

It is possible, though, to read it as a reworking of a familiar pattern and to make connections with, for example, a folktale version of "Little Red Riding Hood"!

■ Before contributing to a class discussion, consider individually how you might complete the following chart with a reading, first, of "How I Contemplated . . . ," and then, of "Little Red Riding Hood."

Pattern?	"How I Contemplated . . ."	"Little Red Riding Hood"
Character leaves home for some reason		To take a basket of food to her grandmother
Character's experiences "out in the world"		
Character has "learning" experience		
Resolution		

Reading Positions

While it is possible to read "How I Contemplated . . ." and "Little Red Riding Hood" for similarities, the reading positions offered to readers appear to be very different.

"Little Red Riding Hood" can be read as offering a lesson: Girls should never stray from the path or something terrible will happen to them. The reader appears to be strongly positioned to produce this reading, although it is possible to resist.

In "How I Contemplated . . . ," although the girl, like Red Riding Hood, "strays from the path" and terrible things happen to her, it is difficult to decide *how* to read events. It is uncertain, for example, whether to read her return home as "A Happy Ending," as the text states. Nor is it easy for readers to decide why the girl shoplifts or becomes involved with Simon. While readers can produce readings of those events—for example, that she acts as she does because her rich parents neglect her—there doesn't appear to be a *stable position* from which readers can make judgments about why characters act as they do.

More Uncertainty?

Conventionally, a distinction is made between what is called first person and third person narration. First person narration is signified by the use of the pronoun "I," where the narrator is both teller and actor "in" the story. The narrator's account, therefore, is assumed to be more personal and subjective than the apparently impersonal and objective mode of third person narration, where the narrator isn't usually a character.

Sometimes, readers might decide that the first person narrator is not to be trusted. Often, the trustworthiness of this first person narrator's account is measured against a third person narration, which readers are invited to accept. But in the case of "How I Contemplated . . . ," the third person narrator is also identified as the first person narrator. The disruption of this narrating convention produces uncertainty for readers.

- Find examples of first and third person narration in "How I Contemplated . . . ," and discuss how they might be read differently. What assumptions might be made about their reliability, for example?

Role Play

One way of exploring how a text is constructed, and possible readings of it, is to try to talk in role—that is, as if you were a character in the story. The point of such an activity might be to:

- produce a reading that includes actions, speeches, even characters that the text does not "provide";
- analyze to what extent the text provides readers with (a) textual fragments or "words on the page" with which to construct a reading, and (b) a stable position from which to read characters and events.

An Example

An interrogator might ask the girl, "Why did you steal and run away?" It is a simple matter to construct or "make up" an answer from already available readings of why a teenage girl might do those things. The text, however, "tells" readers nothing very certain about the girl's reasons for her actions. The impossibility of replying to the question using *only* textual fragments or words on the page tells the reader something about the text's construction and about how readers might produce readings.

If you try to answer a series of questions asked of the girl in a role play, it might help you decide what information (i.e., what words on the page) the text makes available from which to construct a reading of her behavior and motives. It should also raise questions about how readings are produced from minimal or contradictory text information.

■ In your group, try performing one of the following role plays.

An Investigation

In the first part of this activity, you will be able to answer every question, but in the second, where you are trying to point to words on the page, you may not be able to because the questions point to gaps in the text.

■ Complete the girl's replies below. Invent answers you think appropriate on the basis of your reading of the story.

Investigator: You have a big home, don't you?
Girl:
Investigator: Do you like the neighborhood?
Girl:
Investigator: And your parents? Do they treat you well? Give you an allowance?
Girl:
Investigator: A lot of people would say you were a very lucky young lady. [abrupt] Why did you steal the gloves?
Girl:
Investigator: How did your parents react? Were you afraid of them? Was that why you ran away?
Girl:
Investigator: How did you meet Clarita and Simon?
Girl:
Investigator: Describe Clarita to me.
Girl:
Investigator: OK. What kind of a guy was he, this Simon?
Girl:
Investigator: Why did you stay with him?

■ Now, refer to words "on the page" in the story for your answers. (Remember, you may not be able to answer some questions.)

■ You could continue with the investigation. Work in pairs, initially, to write five questions, and then combine with another pair to negotiate on a final list for the investigator to ask the girl.

■ Then, as a group, work on possible answers to your questions.

Remember, your task here is to:

- produce a detailed reading of the girl's behavior and motives;
- compare this reading with one that tries to use only the "words on the page" to construct answers;
- consider where your detailed reading "comes from."

Why This Particular Reading?

- The answers you have written for the girl might suggest that she is unbalanced, a spoiled little rich girl, a sad case, or selfish and self-pitying, all of which are possible readings. It is impossible to prove that any one of these is the correct reading. Why, then, have you produced the reading you have?

An Interview

Another idea is to interview other characters about the girl. In your pair, you might write questions to ask the following characters their opinion of her: (a) Dr. Raymond Forrest and Dr. Coronet; (b) Simon and Clarita; (c) the mother and father; (d) Princess and Dolly.

Refer to the bottom half of the previous page for a suggested guide to organizing your writing and discussion. You might also arrange to perform some of the role plays written by different members of your class.

An Analysis

Alternatively, you could choose two or three brief passages from the text to analyze. A suggested approach is to discuss, and make notes on, the following considerations: (a) possible readings of the passage; (b) the reading position you think is offered to the reader; (c) how reader positioning might be operating (e.g., are there specific words "on the page" that might "activate" particular readings, or might competing readings contribute to a sense of uncertainty?); and (d) why a particular reading might be produced.

An Example

> What a shame, how did it happen?—nothing happened, nothing could have happened, a slight physiological modification known only to a gynecologist or to Dr Coronet. (Part VII, "Events," Passage 4)

One reading of these lines is that the girl was pregnant and that the "slight physiological modification" refers to an abortion. Since powerful readings of abortion as serious and tragic are available in many cultures, the use of the words, "slight physiological modification," foregrounds contradiction.

The position from which to read these lines, therefore, can be one of uncertainty for many readers because it is difficult to decide how to value the words on the page. There is a sense in which readers feel they cannot trust the narrator. Might *she* regard abortion as a "slight physiological modification"? Should the reader? Or should this judgment be attributed to the doctor or her parents? It is not clear. Any choice the reader makes will support particular values and ways of thinking.

- In your group, choose two or three extracts to read and discuss. You might begin with the notes on the "The mother" in Section II, Passage 2. Many readers produce uncomplimentary readings of the character of the mother. You could try to analyze what makes such a reading possible.

3 Intertextuality

Similarities and differences between texts help readers to produce readings. By recognizing relationships between texts and a range of textual possibilities, readers can make predictions, fill gaps, and produce readings.

Different types of stories, or genres, might be said to organize events and characters according to repeated and therefore familiar conventions of story. Such conventions are useful in "locating" readers in relation to a text. The ways in which a text signals its reworking of a familiar pattern can help readers to produce a reading.

The interweaving of texts is called *intertextuality.*

Story conventions are also powerful *social* conventions, which may be why they often seem "natural." By indicating what seem to be more or less acceptable sequences of events, it is as if texts are simply "describing life." For example, these events—"boy meets girl"; "they fall in love"—follow a familiar story convention which readers might assume will conclude in happily "natural" ways. Rather than being natural, however, conventions are *cultural agreements* (which change over time and from place to place) about how and what things might mean.

Thus it is possible to question readings of stories which may seem "natural" and normal by paying attention to the ways a story conforms to or differs from familiar patterns.

In this chapter, you will be asked to consider these issues through your readings of two stories published since 1980. The first, "At Seventeen," could be described as a surfing story, a romance, or perhaps even a fairy tale.

"At Seventeen"

A "surfer" is assumed to surf waves, usually with a board. It is also a word that can suggest to many readers a range of readings of the participants' appearance and habits, as well as their class, race, and gender.

- With a partner, spend a few minutes jotting down the readings that are suggested to you by the word "surfer" or "surfie" before reading the story "At Seventeen," which follows. Include as many details as you can—appearance, clothing, speech, habits, and so on.

At Seventeen

Sheila Morehead

The youth shivered as the cool breeze flicked around his body and blew through his sea-bleached hair. His eyes, darkly blue as the glowering sky above, turned continually to the heaving surf.

There was no one else on the windswept beach. Inside his mind a voice was talking to him and that voice was his own soul and it was all the companionship necessary to him.

"I am free," he told his inner voice. "Yes, you are free," was the reply. And he stared down at his hands, examined the long thin fingers, and smiled.

In answer to his smile the sun escaped over the rim of a cloud, electrifying the black edges with a white, bright band. The wind paused and his body warmed on the instant.

An ant laboured across his toes tugging a dead beetle three times its size over the brown mounds of skin and bone. The youth, when the ant had crossed the barriers safely, heaved himself to his feet, bent to swoop up his board and jogged down to the sea. He went into the surf and let the thunder of its voice drown out his own secret one; and he emptied his mind into the ocean.

That was Monday.

On Tuesday he again chose to sit all morning on the beach. He sat outside his tent and the only sound was the whine of the wind and the crash and hiss of the sea as it surged across the bank of sand to form the even steady tubes he'd come so far to ride.

This day he remembered the first time he'd ever used a surf-board. He'd been nine years old and he'd been taken for a holiday to the east coast. His board had been white and made of foam and he frowned as he felt once more the harsh scratch of its surface on his chest. He'd worn a T-shirt the next day, but it had made no difference. So he'd tried to stand and he had stood and he'd begun to learn to be a surfer and he knew, even then, that he had found something very special to himself.

The sets, this Tuesday afternoon, were big. Very big and very frightening and he rode them because he had to. Because they were there. And he found himself crying with fear as his board ripped off the strapping of his ankle rope and allowed the ocean to toss him off its crests and roll him, in suffocating somersaults, on the grit beneath. Gasping, he floundered to the shore and then once more lay along his board and fought his way out.

Wednesday. And the sound of an engine revving over the narrow sandy strip he'd earlier forced his bike over with the same urgent sound.

Over the last dune the youth watched the black moving speck grow to a denim-clad figure sitting, as he himself had sat, astride a scarlet 'glass board. The shine was still on it; no dull worms of wax straggled across its immaculate surface.

Sweet God! There'd be beer cans in the haversacks slung from either side of the bike. And a transistor in the pack on the surfie's back. Because he was what he was he would be affable, sit over a camp fire smoking dope he didn't need and drinking beer he didn't want. For there was no time left from his week to find another solitary surf-perfect beach.

The newcomer hadn't seen him yet. The sun-tanned circle of his face was concentrating on the soft ground beneath his wheels. That face would split into a grin when it saw him lying there. The mouth would say "Hi!" and his would say "Hi!" and then "What's it like out there?" and "Where you from?" and on and on into the last moments of his one week of freedom.

That's it then, the youth thought as the face lifted and two grey eyes swept the beach and riveted on himself and his board and his bike.

But there was no wide grin, no opening of a mouth. Just a cooling of the eyes and a creasing of smooth forehead and then a rev of engine as the rider headed the bike to the farthest point of the short crescent of beach.

The youth took his board and surfed himself out in the green waves and when he returned the stranger's tent was pitched and there was no movement. He lit a small fire and heated a can of soup.

When he rose to scatter the fire, the figure walking towards the beach—board now daubed and criss-crossed expertly with wax—was not that of a man. The black and purple wet suit moulded itself around swelling breasts and rounded hips and hugged a small, hand-span waist.

The youth slept fitfully that night. The wail of the sea seemed to taunt him. "No escape," it cried. "You are one of many. Only I am one."

In the early morning of the following day, he sat in his tent and waxed his board. He felt feverish. He felt that the hurt of his loss of solitude, time to be himself, had damaged him physically as well as spiritually.

Brooding, he went into the waiting sea and battled through the screaming waves. He was cold, colder than he should be; and his wet suit, gaping at one sleeve join, leaked in the icy ocean. He looked back, gauging the waves, and he saw the girl, black-clad, sitting outside her tent, a long red mark on the sand beside her.

He brought his leg up onto the board and peeled off the ankle rope. Beneath was scoured skin, too painful to take the pull and snap when and if the surf disposed of him.

Then he turned his board to shore and dug his hands into the ocean as a mighty swell lifted him and the makings of a king wave began.

Too big! Too strong! He was off his board, free-falling into a cavern of sand-splattered green and his sun-yellow board was flung up and away from him. He tried to swim as he surfaced but sudden cramp clutched at his leg and his body wouldn't respond to the urging of his brain.

He was lifted again and he saw the girl. She was standing now, motionless. She would not come, on her scarlet board, until he raised his arm.

But he would not signal. He would not!

And the girl wouldn't move. It never occurred to him that she dare not come. She was a surfer. He knew she was waiting. Waiting because she couldn't be sure, wouldn't mock him by offering help because he struggled.

The sea swirled in his mouth. His sun-scoured hair, long and thick and wet-dark-gold, floated round his head and he blinked rapidly as he tried to rid his eyes of the salt water.

He knew that if the girl didn't come, he would die.

Beaten, sobbing with the shame he felt, he held his arm above him as the sea lifted him again, and he saw the girl bend and take her board off the sand and begin to move to the water.

As the water bubbled down his throat he knew that he was dying where he had always believed he would want to die . . . but it was too soon, too soon!

When the girl reached him she shoved her board under his arm and grabbed at his hair and over the sound of the sea he heard her shout, "We're going back together."

Through the tumbling, roaring surf the girl never lost her hold on his hair, her hand was bunched in it, her fingers locked in it, until she and her blood red board and the half-dead youth were spewed up on the sand.

She dropped her board then and dragged him up the sand to her tent and she zipped open her sleeping bag and wrapped him in it. She piled a blanket on him and got his sleeping bag and spread that on top of him and then she made a fire close by. When she'd finished she lay down beside him and worked her way under the coverings and pressed herself close to him and after a while he felt a faint warmth begin to unlock the chill of his body, and he slept.

Friday. A pale sun in a clear sky was already warming the sand when he opened his eyes.

He lifted his head and she was sitting cross-legged on the sand beside him.

Her grey eyes were still cool. They looked straight into his as he raised himself slightly.

"Thanks," was all he could find to say.

"That's all right," she replied and stopped looking at him and turned her eyes to the sea.

Then she continued, "I'll go. This is your beach."

Mid-day he watched her, from his own tent, pack. As she laid her board along her bike and straddled it and started the engine he stood and walked to her.

"Thanks," he said again. And because he felt he had to say it he continued very softly, "I didn't want you here, you know."

She shrugged. "I was in trouble once," she said. "I left it until the last seconds too. I knew how you felt."

She put the bike into gear and moved up the sand, the board glowing dark red beneath her.

The youth began to dismantle his tent, began to pack his haversack, then he too left the beach behind.

When he reached the highway he opened the tail-gate of his P-plated, rust-filigreed wagon and ran his bike up a plank.

He glanced at the track her car had left in the sandy edges of the road and although it was not the way he'd planned to go he swung his car around, and followed.

Before and After

- In your group, briefly summarize what you consider to be the reading promoted by "At Seventeen" of "the surfer."
- In a class discussion, compare the readings produced in your class *before* and *after* reading "At Seventeen," in terms of:
  - how similar the readings are;
  - how different the readings are;
  - how you would account for the production of these particular readings of surfers in the class;
  - how the readings produced in your class are confirmed or challenged by the reading apparently promoted by "At Seventeen";
  - whether, and if so how, readings of "the surfer" as white and male tend to dominate in a sport which includes many women and first became popular in the islands of the Pacific Ocean.

A Fairy Tale?

As well as drawing on available texts about, and readings of, surfers, "At Seventeen" can be read to parallel a traditional fairy tale.

- The left column of the following chart lists a number of conventional fairy tale events. Below the chart are suggested parallels for how the events of "At Seventeen" might be read and matched. Copy the chart and complete it with a partner before comparing decisions, first with another pair, and then in a class discussion.

Fairy Tale	"At Seventeen"
Princess in tower	Boy alone on beach
Prince arrives on a horse	
Princess spinning at window	
Prince sees her, climbs tower, rescues her	
Princess thanks him	

Possible Parallels

Boy thanks her.
Boy surfing, gets into difficulties.
Girl watches and then saves him.
Boy alone on beach.
Girl arrives on a motorbike.
Girl surfing, gets into difficulties.
Boy watches and then saves her.
Girl thanks him.

A Fairy Tale Ending?

To this point in the story, it seems possible to compare events to a familiar fairy tale pattern, with the sex and gender reversed to create the following pairings: boy = princess, and girl = prince. To continue the parallel, the modern prince, who in "At Seventeen" is the female character, should ask the "princess" (the boy) for a date or, in some way, pursue him to a happy ending. But how does "At Seventeen" continue?

■ As a class, discuss possible reasons for "At Seventeen" concluding with *another* reversal of gender roles. Then read the section below.

Stories as Social Regulation

One idea is that stories can act as a form of social regulation by supporting some ways of thinking and disqualifying others. This might mean that stories are most readily read in ways which support dominant or traditional ideas.

Stories might also try, however, to support or promote ideas or ways of thinking that are, in some sense, alternative—that is, ways of thinking that might be alternative or resistant to dominant ideas.

There are, for example, competing ways of thinking about what it is to be "masculine" or "feminine." "At Seventeen" might be read as promoting alternative views to traditional ways of thinking about masculinity and femininity. The girl and boy could be seen as "transgressing" boundaries of "appropriate" masculine and feminine behavior. He is gentle, introspective, and not self-sufficient in the scene; she is independent and saves him.

When characters "transgress" traditional gender boundaries of a particular culture, they are often "punished" in some way. In fairy tales, for example, the witch and the "henpecked husband" transgress boundaries in certain ways and thus are read as, respectively, wicked and weak. "At Seventeen" supports some "transgressions." But then the genders are reversed again to follow a traditional pattern:

Fairy Tale	**"At Seventeen"**
Prince asks for her hand in marriage.	Girl (now the princess?) leaves. The boy (now the prince?) follows.
They live happily ever after.	And . . .

If the text had the boy leave and the girl follow, would this be too much of a transgression in terms of gender? It might risk a negative reading of the girl as "unfeminine" (expressed in terms, perhaps, which question her morals). The boy could be at risk too. He could be read as "unmasculine" for not taking the initiative. He can be saved by the girl and, in some readings at least, remain masculine enough, but if he continues to be the passive partner in the duo, does he risk being read as weak and not a "real" man?

Writing Beyond the Ending

Conventional ideas about romance make certain sets of narrative conventions possible and other sets less possible. For example, falling in love and getting married is only *one* of a number of options open to women. Romantic stories, however, actively promote this option as a "natural" choice.

If "At Seventeen" had concluded with the girl following the boy, then readers' narrative expectations might have been disrupted. Similarly, if the story ended without the expectation of a continuing relationship between the girl and boy, (in "real life" not every meeting leads to love), it could seem unusual in a way that his following her does not. To most readers, it is clear why he's following and it is not difficult to predict an ending.

■ Write two endings to "At Seventeen" that begin where the text you have read concludes. One ending should conform to conventions of a romantic story, while the other should challenge conventions.

"A Blow, a Kiss"

"A Blow, a Kiss" was written by a Western Australian writer, Tim Winton, and published in 1985 in an anthology titled *Scission.*

It has been described as an Australian "mateship" story and read as following a familiar pattern. Alone with nature, characters, generally male, face a situation which requires great courage, but leads to the characters developing insights about themselves and about each other, and results in their forming a special bond.

"A Blow, a Kiss" has also been called a boy's "coming of age" story. An event in a boy's life is read as moving him out of childhood and into adulthood.

Many "coming of age" stories read in classrooms are about white male characters. One could ask, Why is that the case? and Whose interests are served by that selection?

Traditional ways of thinking about mateship and coming of age (like ways of thinking about romance) make certain sets of narrative conventions more likely in a story. Particular options and relationships are promoted as "natural" and even universal, which is one of the ways in which the predominance of stories about white male characters is defended. It is said that the race, class, and gender of characters don't really matter, because readers are reading about the "human condition," which is universal.

■ As you read "A Blow, a Kiss," ask yourself whether or not this story could have been written with a mother and daughter for the central characters instead of a father and son. (Line numbers are included in the story to help you with an activity after you read it.)

A Blow, a Kiss

Tim Winton

Despite their bad luck, Albie had enjoyed the night. Just the pipe smell of his father and the warmth of him in the truck's cab beside him was enough. It did not matter that they had caught ten salmon and buried them in the sand for safekeeping and not found them again. The Tilley lamp tinkled, cooling between his feet on the floor of the cab. Ahead, the unlit road rolled out.

A motorcycle whipped past, going their way. Albie saw the small red light for a moment and then it was gone.

"He's flying," his father murmured.

"Yeah." Albie felt his chin on his chest. He heard the lamp tinkle. His eyes closed. He looked up again, felt himself plummeting forward, heard his father pumping the brakes.

"He's down!" bellowed his father.

Albie pulled himself away from the windscreen. His father was already out of the cab and in the vortex of the headlights. On the road, the motorcycle was sprawled, intertwined with the rider, an ugly spillage. Against the blackness of machine and leather, Albie saw blood. He did not move on the seat. He held the Tilley lamp hard between his feet, he had not let it fall and break.

His father pulled the machine from the man who groaned. He took the helmet off. He held the man's hands. They were the colour of bleeding pork. Albie had never seen so much human blood, though he had seen cut pigs and the jugulars of salmon cannoning red on white sand. Groans became shouts. Without warning, the fallen man lashed out at Albie's father and pulled him down to the ground by the ears and the two men locked limbs, and rolled on the bloody bitumen in the headlights of the truck. Albie did not move. He held the Tilley lamp tight until his thighs ached. He heard the wet sound of fists connecting. Crickets and the quiet idle of the engine underlay this noise. Beyond the grovelling men, past the point of the truck's headlights, there was only darkness. In a moment there was quiet. Crickets chanted. The engine idled.

"Albie!"

Albie slid out of the cab as soon as he heard his father's voice. Every line and feature was stark in the glare. Blood ran from his father's lips. The fallen rider lay, gored jaws apart, beneath him.

"Come here, Albie." His father motioned with a free hand. Albie smelt blood, and beer and petrol and hot metal. He saw a translucent disc on his father's cheek and for a moment he thought it was a tear but it was a fish scale. "He's unconscious. We shouldn't move him. I'll have to call for help. Come over further. Now get on him." Albie was astride the bleeding, still man. "Put your feet on his hands. He won't move. He's out." Albie wondered why it was necessary to sit on a man who was not going to move. He looked at the blood

40 streaming from his father's lips. "He's in shock—he didn't know what he was doing," his father said. "I won't be long—stay put."

Albie felt his shoulder briefly squeezed and heard his father's boots mashing back to the truck. The lights veered from him and the truck passed and the tail-lights became tiny red points, eyes that closed and left him with the dark. He heard the man's breathing, felt the rise and fall of leather, listened to the cricket hymns, wondering what should be done, how he should behave towards this man who had struck his father. In the dark, he could not see the places where skin had been pared away. He saw no human blood, but he could smell it.

50 "He was only helping you," he said to the man. The leather jacket groaned beneath him. Albie wondered what his mother would be doing. Probably ringing Sergeant Fobles, he thought; she'll be angry and blame Dad, kiss us. Albie knew she would use her kisses like blows: punishment for them.

The leather jacket was wet in parts and torn. It shocked him that leather should rip like that; it was the strongest stuff there was, and only time and sweat and constant fatigue could waste it, not those few seconds when that single tail-light disappeared and this man skittered along the road like a moist piece of moss.

"You're lucky we were here," he said, shifting position on the mount. "You're
60 lucky my Dad's going for help."

Town was only twenty minutes' drive from the coast. Farmland stretched right to the high water mark. Albie had seen cattle on the beaches, wallowing in the surf. He hoped his father found a farm with a phone.

"Come on, Dad. Come on, Dad. Come on, Dad." He often prayed to his father in his absence. God, he decided, was just like his Dad, only bigger. It was easier to pray to him and hope God got the message on relay.

"Dad?"

Albie flinched. The injured man had spoken.

"Dad?"

70 Albie's body shrank into itself. He waited for the man to move, to attack.

"Dad?"

"Yes?" Albie whispered. His throat was full of heart.

"Oh. Oh, Dad, I'm sorry. Was coming back."

Albie listened as the man began to weep; he rode the man's sobs high on his chest, and it hurt him to hear. Like the sound of a tractor engine turning over on a dying battery.

"It's alright," Albie said to him, "it's alright." The sobbing continued, jogging him, making the leather groan and the seat of his pants hot until Albie thought he might be sick or get up and run away into the bush at the side of the road.

80 But he did not run. He bent down and kissed the wet, prickled face. The sobbing stopped. Even the crickets paused. Albie tasted salt, felt a jumble of things lurching in him; he felt not sick, just full.

It was that moment when Albie began to worry that the man might die.

The lights forking out over the crown of the hill took him by surprise. He watched them dip and sweep, disappear and reappear until he could hear the sound of the truck's engine.

In the piercing white light of the truck's lamps, as it stopped dead with a shriek of brakes, Albie knew what it must be to be a rabbit, powerless, snowblind, vulnerable to atrocity. The light seemed to ricochet inside his
90 head, confounding him. He heard his father's boots.

"You alright? There's blood on your face!"

Albie felt himself swept up into his father's arms; he yielded to it. His father hugged him, touched his cheeks with his fingers and his tobacco breath. On his own feet again, Albie found his voice and asked, "Is he going to die?"

"Dunno," his father said. "I don't know enough about it."

"Oh."

"There's no phones. I should've known in the first place. Man'd have to be an idiot. We'll take him in ourselves like we should've anyhow."

"We didn't want to move him."

100 "Yeah." His father seemed to take comfort in this.

Albie tried to stay awake in the warm cab, seduced by the smell of his father and the crooning note of the engine. The sweat had dried on him. His arms still ached. He had never lifted anything so heavy, so awkward as that fallen motorcyclist. They had tried to get his contorted, cold machine in too, but had to leave it at the roadside. Every few minutes, Albie turned to see through the window the shape of the injured man beneath the tarpaulin on the tray beside the rods and sacks and engine parts.

He held the Tilley lamp hard between his heels. It kept him awake, a duty.

"Should've known better," his father muttered. The featureless road wandered
110 left and right, studded with the eyes of beer cans, mile pegs, rabbits.

Somewhere in his fog of fatigue, Albie hoped his mother would understand. She loved them; she didn't like them to be late.

Town was mostly asleep at this time of night. Only the pub and the petrol station were open. It was a fuel town at night, a farm town by day. As they pulled into the sudden brilliance of the petrol station tarmac, Albie saw Mr. Stevens wave to his father; a wave without hands. His father got out. After a moment, Mr. Stevens came over. Albie listened.

"That's Wilf Beacon's boy," Mr. Stevens said, peering in the back at the man on the tray beneath the tarp. "Dead?"

120 Albie wished his father would check. He was afraid. But he saw the tarp rising and falling.

"Where's Beacon, then?"

"Across the road."

Albie knew that in this town "across the road" meant in the pub. The pub frightened Albie. From out on the verandah, it was a roar, a sour smell, unknown.

Not long after, Albie saw two men stumble out onto the pub verandah. One was his father. The other man had him by the throat and his father had the man's forelock in his fist. Shouting, Albie saw his father hit the man in the
130 chest. The man fell to his knees. His father helped him up and they came across the road to Stevens' Garage.

"Just pull yourself together," he heard his father say with a harshness that made his skin prickle.

"Where's his suitcase? He had a sleeping bag! You've done him over! What've you been doin' to my boy?"

"Pickin' him up off the side of the road. He's drunk like you. He's hurt, you bloody idiot!"

Albie hated that man. He couldn't remember seeing him before. He was not a farmer. Might have been a farm hand for someone he didn't know. He didn't
140 care; he hated him. He wanted the man to see his son, and to weep like the son had wept out on the road with that hopeless starter motor sound in the dark.

His father shoved the man around to the back of the truck. Albie's insteps were cold from pressing against the lamp. He watched through the grimy little back window. The man staggered up onto the tray and knelt with a thud beside the body under the tarp.

"Little coward. Leave a man alone. Own father. Own father." The rider's bloody face was immobile. The old man's hands touched it, lifted the head off the truck tray. "And what've yer got to say for yerself? They bring yer back to *me*!" The sound of the rider's head being dropped onto the metal tray vibrated
150 through the whole truck like the sound of a mallee root being tossed in. Again. Whump. The father beat his son's head against the tray. Albie's father looked helpless, did not move.

Albie got out. The flat bed of the truck resounded again. The jumble inside Albie pushed upward; he wanted to be sick. He snatched the Tilley lamp by the handle. He heard the startled voice of his father. He swung the lamp up and over; a bowling movement. Glass and sound and splintery light happened all at once and his father had hold of him as the drunk old man lay still on his son, stinking of beer and kerosene.

160 As they turned off the bitumen road into their own run of gravel to the yellow-lit house down in the valley, Albie ended the silence with a question. He was startled by his own toneless delivery.

"Why did that man hit his son for getting hurt?"

His father sighed. He sounded relieved that the silence was finished. "I don't know, boy."

"Would you do that to me?"

The truck slewed and stopped.

"Lord, no. God A'mighty, no!"

"He was going home," Albie said.

170 His father's mouth moved. He reached out and put his knuckles to Albie's cheek, left them there for a long time, as though still waiting for words to come. "Sorry about the salmon," he said at last, "I should've known better."

The truck moved forward again. Albie felt those knuckles on his cheek still and knew, full to bursting, that that was how God would touch someone. He neither moved nor spoke, and the truck trundled on.

Blows and Kisses

- Individually, write a short paragraph describing your reading of "A Blow, a Kiss," in terms of what you think it is about, and how you read the characters.
- Compare readings in a class discussion, before starting the following activities.
- In your pair, decide who is doing what to whom, by completing the chart below. The first line has been filled in for you.

Character	A Blow	A Kiss
Albie	Hits bike rider's father	Kisses bike rider
Albie's father		
Albie's mother		
Bike rider		
Wilf Beacon		

- Assume that you live in a society that subscribes to the belief that people should kiss one another rather than hit one another. Look at the chart and decide which of the characters' behavior would be privileged or approved of by this society. List these characters.
- In your group, compare the lists that you have compiled, and make any additions or deletions that you think necessary.
- Discuss whether the text appears to support the view that people should kiss one another rather than hit one another.

Selecting a Reading

In the left column of Figure 1 below, lines from the story are listed opposite statements which summarize sometimes-contradictory readings of those lines.

- In your pair, select one or two statements from each section on the right which are closest to your reading of each set of lines in the left-hand column. Record the numbers of the statements you select to compare in your group.

Extracts	Statements
Albie wondered why it was necessary to sit on a man who was not going to move. (line 38) "Dunno," his father said, "I don't know enough about it." (line 95) "There's no phones. I should've known better in the first place. Man'd have to be an idiot. We'll take him in ourselves like we should've anyhow." (line 97) "Should've known better," his father muttered. (line 109)	1. Albie obeys his father because his father always knows best. 2. Whenever there is a decision to be made, Albie's father is confused about what to do. 3. Albie's father is kind-hearted and does the best he can under the circumstances. 4. Albie's father is not able to answer his son's questions. 5. Albie's father is a good role model for his son.
Albie wondered what his mother would be doing. Probably ringing Sergeant Fobles. . . ." (line 51) Albie knew she would use her kisses like blows: punishment for them. (line 53) Albie hoped his mother would understand. (line 111)	6. Albie is afraid of his mother. 7. Men seem tough but are really gentle. Women seem gentle but are really tough. 8. Albie's mother overreacts. 9. Albie's mother quite understandably would be anxious about their lateness.
He bent down and kissed the wet, prickled face. (line 80) "Would you do that to me?" (line 165) He reached out and put his knuckles to Albie's cheek, left them there for a long time, as though still waiting for words to come. (line 169)	10. Albie's father finds it hard to express gentle emotions. 11. Depending on the situation, Albie's father is able to be gentle or tough. 12. Albie shows his feelings too much. 13. Albie is not afraid of his father, who is gentle.
. . . the two men locked limbs, and rolled on the bloody bitumen. . . . (line 23) He heard the wet sound of fists connecting. (line 25) Shouting, Albie saw his father hit the man on the chest. (line 129) The father beat his son's head against the tray. (line 151) He swung the lamp up and over; a bowling movement. (line 155)	14. The descriptions of violence in this story are unnecessarily graphic. 15. Men's lives involve violence and physical toughness so this should be represented in a story such as this. 16. Albie by the end has become a man; he's learned to hit as well as to kiss. 17. Sometimes it's necessary to hit people even if they are old and drunk, or injured. 18. Albie's father hits people a lot even if they are old and drunk, or injured.

Figure 1

Constructing a Reading in Support Of?

Your selection of statements should help you to describe a certain reading of the story. For instance, if you have selected statements 2, 4, 9, 10, 14, and 18, then you will have constructed a reading of the story which is in opposition to a selection of, say, 3, 5, 6, 7, 11, 15, and 17.

- Of the list of possible readings below, decide in your group which readings are best supported by each pair's selection of statements.

  a. Albie's father is a tough and violent man who is adored by his gentle son. Finally, he teaches his son that there are times when a man must hit other people because they deserve to be hit or because that is the only way to communicate with them.
  b. Albie learns from his sensitive father that despite the violence of life there are important times for tenderness. Their experiences draw them closer together.
  c. Albie knows that men lead different lives from women and that they communicate in more direct ways. Women may appear to be gentle even though they can be quite violent, while men may appear to be violent but are sensitive and caring people underneath the toughness.
  d. Stories about men often portray violence as a necessary part of life and present a view of men as being in charge of the events in which they are involved. This story is no different in that respect. Albie's father uses violence when necessary and takes charge of situations without difficulty.
  e. Stories about men often portray violence as a necessary part of life and present a view of men as being in charge of the events in which they are involved. This story is of this genre, although Albie's father could be viewed as using violence gratuitously while making silly decisions about particular actions and events.

- When you have decided which of the above readings best matches each pair's selection of statements, discuss how it compares to the readings you each wrote about before beginning these activities.

Class Discussion

1. In what ways has "A Blow, a Kiss" been read similarly by members of your class?
2. In what ways has "A Blow, a Kiss" been read differently by members of your class?
3. How would you account for any similarities between the readings constructed of "A Blow, a Kiss" in your class?
4. How would you account for any differences between the readings constructed of "A Blow, a Kiss" in your class?

4 Rereadings?

As we have investigated so far, readers do not always produce or construct the same readings of texts. This book argues that this is *no*t because readers, influenced by their personal experiences, produce uniquely individual readings.

Both writers and readers appear to produce a limited *range of meanings* rather than millions of uniquely different readings. The meanings or readings produced by readers (and writers) aren't just thought up by individuals, but are ways of thinking that are available in a particular culture at certain times and places.

Readings or meanings that are powerful in particular cultures or societies are called *dominant readings.* Often, these are almost invisible as readings because they are so taken for granted that they seem "natural" or real. In other cultures, however, or at other times, these readings may seem quite strange.

There is no such thing as a neutral or objective reading: readings always affirm or support certain beliefs and values and always benefit particular groups of people. Sometimes, groups of people, both readers and writers, resist what may be a dominant reading. They *reread* dominant readings and attempt to promote *rereadings* which support different values.

The stories in this chapter might both be read as promoting rereadings in some senses. That is, they could be argued (a) to resist particular dominant readings, and (b) to invite rereadings.

Sometimes readers become aware of a dominant reading only when it is challenged. In this chapter you will be asked to consider:

- how and why readers might resist dominant readings of texts;
- how and why readers might reread particular texts;
- how and why texts might appear to promote rereadings.

"The Lottery"

The story that follows is called "The Lottery." It is set in an Australian city a few years after the Great Depression in the 1930s. The amount won in the lottery is five thousand pounds, which was considered a small fortune in those days.

- As you near the end of the story, you will encounter a pause in the narrative. At that point, spend a few minutes in your group discussing how you think the story will end. Make brief notes about your prediction to share with the rest of the class. Then, read the ending written by Marjorie Barnard.

The Lottery

Marjorie Barnard

The first that Ted Bilborough knew of his wife's good fortune was when one of his friends, an elderly wag, shook his hand with mock gravity and murmured a few words of manly but inappropriate sympathy. Ted didn't know what to make of it. He had just stepped from the stairway on to the upper deck of the 6:15 P.M. ferry from town. Fred Lewis seemed to have been waiting for him, and as he looked about he got the impression of newspapers and grins and a little flutter of half derisive excitement, all focused on himself. Everything seemed to bulge towards him. It must be some sort of leg pull. He felt his assurance threatened, and the corner of his mouth twitched uncomfortably in his fat cheek, as he tried to assume a hard boiled manner.

"Keep the change, laddie," he said.

"He doesn't know, actually he doesn't know."

"Your wife's won the lottery!"

"He won't believe you. Show him the paper. There it is as plain as my nose. Mrs. Grace Bilborough, 52 Cuthbert Street." A thick, stained forefinger pointed to the words. "First prize, five thousand pounds, Last Hope Syndicate."

"He's taking it very hard," said Fred Lewis, shaking his head.

They began thumping him on the back. He had travelled on the ferry every week-day for the last ten years, barring a fortnight's holiday in January, and he knew nearly everyone. Even those he didn't know entered into the spirit of it. Ted filled his pipe nonchalantly but with unsteady fingers. He was keeping that odd unsteadiness, that seemed to begin somewhere deep in his chest, to himself. It was a wonder that fellows in the office hadn't got hold of this, but they had been busy today in the hot loft under the chromium pipes of the pneumatic system, sending down change and checking up on credit accounts. Sale time. Grace might have let him know. She could have rung up from Thompson's. Bill was always borrowing the lawn mower and the step ladder, so it would hardly be asking a favour in the circumstances. But that was Grace all over.

"If I can't have it myself, you're the man I like to see get it."

They meant it too. Everyone liked Ted in a kind sort of way. He was a good fellow in both senses of the word. Not namby pamby, always ready for a joke but a good citizen too, a good husband and father. He wasn't the sort that refused to wheel the perambulator.[1] He flourished the perambulator. His wife could hold up her head, they paid their bills weekly and he even put something away, not much but something, and that was a triumph the way things were, the ten per cent knocked off his salary in the depression not restored yet, and one thing and another. And always cheerful, with a joke for everyone. All this was vaguely present in Ted's mind. He'd always expected in a trusting sort of way to be rewarded, but not through Grace.

---

1. *Perambulator:* baby carriage.

"What are you going to do with it, Ted?"

"You won't see him for a week, he's going on a jag." This was very funny because Ted never did, not even on Anzac Day.[2]

A voice with a grievance said, not for the first time, "I've had shares in a ticket every week since it started, and I've never won a cent." No one was interested.

"You'll be going off on a trip somewhere?"

"They'll make you president of the Tennis Club and you'll have to donate a silver cup."

They were flattering him underneath the jokes.

"I expect Mrs. Bilborough will want to put some of it away for the children's future," he said. It was almost as if he was giving an interview to the press, and he was pleased with himself for saying the right thing. He always referred to Grace in public as Mrs. Bilborough. He had too nice a social sense to say "the Missus."

Ted let them talk, and looked out of the window. He wasn't interested in the news in the paper tonight. The little boat vibrated fussily, and left a long wake like moulding glass in the quiet river. The evening was drawing in. The sun was sinking into a bank of grey cloud, soft and formless as mist. The air was dusky, so that its light was closed into itself and it was easy to look at, a thick golden disc more like a moon rising through the smoke than the sun. It threw a single column of orange light on the river, the ripples from the ferry fanned out into it, and their tiny shadows truncated it. The bank, rising steeply from the river and closing it in till it looked like a lake, was already bloomed with shadows.

"Five thousand pounds," he thought. "Five thousand pounds." Five thousand pounds stewing gently in its interest, making old age safe. He could do almost anything he could think of with five thousand pounds. It gave his mind a stretched sort of feeling, just to think of it. It was hard to connect five thousand pounds with Grace. She might have let him know. And where had the five and threepence to buy the ticket come from? He couldn't help wondering about that. When you budgeted as carefully as they did there wasn't five and threepence over. If there had been, well, it wouldn't have been over at all, he would have put it in the bank. He hadn't noticed any difference in the housekeeping, and he prided himself he noticed everything. Surely she hadn't been running up bills to buy lottery tickets. His mind darted here and there suspiciously. There was something secretive in Grace, and he'd thought she told him everything. He'd taken it for granted, only, of course, in the ordinary run there was nothing to tell. He consciously relaxed the knot in his mind. After all, Grace had won the five thousand pounds. He remembered charitably that she had always been a good wife to him. As he thought that he had a vision of the patch on his shirt, his newly washed cream trousers laid out for tennis, the children's neatness, the tidy house. That was being a good wife. And he had been a good husband, always brought his money home and never looked at

2. Anzac Day is an annual remembrance of soldiers and noncombatants from Australia and New Zealand who have served and died in wars from World War I onward.

another woman. Theirs was a model home, everyone acknowledged it, but—well—somehow he found it easier to be cheerful in other people's homes than in his own. It was Grace's fault. She wasn't cheery and easy going. Something moody about her now. Woody. He'd worn better than Grace, anyone could see that, and yet it was he who had had the hard time. All she had to do was to stay at home and look after the house and the children. Nothing much in that. She always seemed to be working, but he couldn't see what there was to do that could take her so long. Just a touch of woman's perversity. It wasn't that Grace had aged. Ten years married and with two children, there was still something girlish about her—raw, hard girlishness that had never mellowed. Maybe she'd be a bit brighter now. He could not help wondering how she had managed the five and three. If she could shower five and threes about like that, he'd been giving her too much for the housekeeping. And why did she want to give it that damnfool name, "Last Hope." That meant there had been others, didn't it? It probably didn't mean a thing, just a lucky tag.

A girl on the seat opposite was sewing lace on silkies for her trousseau, working intently in the bad light.

"Another one starting out," Ted thought.

"What about it?" said the man beside him.

Ted hadn't been listening.

The ferry had tied up at his landing stage and Ted got off. He tried not to show in his walk that his wife had won five thousand pounds. He felt jaunty and tired at once. He walked up the hill with a bunch of other men, his neighbours. They were still teasing him about the money, they didn't know how to stop. It was a very still, warm evening. As the sun descended into the misty bank on the horizon it picked out the delicate shapes of clouds invisibly sunk in the mass, outlining them with a fine thread of gold.

One by one the men dropped out, turning into side streets or opening garden gates till Ted was alone with a single companion, a man who lived in a semi-detached cottage at the end of the street. They were suddenly very quiet and sober. Ted felt the ache around his mouth where he'd been smiling and smiling.

"I'm awfully glad you've had this bit of luck."

"I'm sure you are, Eric," Ted answered in a subdued voice.

"There's nobody I'd sooner see have it."

"That's very decent of you."

"I mean it."

"Well, well, I wasn't looking for it."

"We could do with a bit of luck like that in our house."

"I bet you could."

"There's an instalment on the house due next month, and Nellie's got to come home again. Bob can't get anything to do. Seems as if we'd hardly done paying for the wedding."

"That's bad."

"She's expecting, so I suppose Mum and Dad will be let in for all that too."

"It seems only the other day Nellie was a kid getting round on a scooter."

"They grow up," Eric agreed. "It's the instalment that's the rub. First of next month. They expect it on the nail too. If we hadn't that hanging over us it wouldn't matter about Nellie coming home. She's our girl, and it'll be nice to have her about the place again."

"You'll be proud as a cow with two tails when you're a grandpa."

"I suppose so."

They stood mutely by Eric's gate. An idea began to flicker in Ted's mind, and with it came a feeling of sweetness and happiness and power such as he had never expected to feel.

"I won't see you stuck, old man," he said.

"That's awfully decent of you."

"I mean it."

They shook hands as they parted. Ted had only a few steps more and he took them slowly. Very warm and dry, he thought. The garden will need watering. Now he was at his gate. There was no one in sight. He stood for a moment looking about him. It was as if he saw the house he had lived in for ten years, for the first time. He saw that it had a mean, narrow-chested appearance. The roof tiles were discoloured, the woodwork needed painting, the crazy pavement that he had laid with such zeal had an unpleasant flirtatious look. The revolutionary thought moved in his mind, "We might leave here." Measured against the possibilities that lay before him, it looked small and mean. Even the name, "Emoh Ruo" seemed wrong, pokey.

Ted was reluctant to go in. It was so long since anything of the least importance had happened between him and Grace, that it made him shy. He did not know how she would take it. Would she be all in a dither and no dinner ready? He hoped so but feared not.

He went into the hall, hung up his hat and shouted in a big bluff voice, "Well, well, well, and where's my rich wife?"

* * * *

Grace was in the kitchen dishing up dinner.

"You're late," she said. "The dinner's spoiling."

The children were quiet but restless, anxious to leave the table and go out to play. "I got rid of the reporters," Grace said in a flat voice. Grace had character, trust her to handle a couple of cub reporters. She didn't seem to want to talk about it to her husband either. He felt himself, his voice, his stature dwindling. He looked at her with hard eyes. "Where did she get the money," he wondered again, but more sharply.

Presently they were alone. There was a pause. Grace began to clear the table. Ted felt that he must do something. He took her awkwardly into his arms. "Gracie, aren't you pleased?"

She stared at him a second then her face seemed to fall together, a sort of spasm, something worse than tears. But she twitched away from him. "Yes," she said, picking up a pile of crockery and making for the kitchen. He followed her.

"You're a dark horse, never telling me a word about it."

"She's like ice," he thought.

She moved about the kitchen with quick nervous movements. After a moment, she answered what was in his mind:

"I sold mother's ring and chain. A man came to the door buying old gold. I bought a ticket every week till the money was gone."

"Oh," he said. Grace had sold her mother's wedding ring to buy a lottery ticket.

"It was my money."

"I didn't say it wasn't."

"No, you didn't."

The plates chattered in her hands. She was evidently feeling something, and feeling it strongly. But Ted didn't know what. He couldn't make her out.

She came and stood in front of him, her back to the littered table, her whole body taut. "I suppose you're wondering what I'm going to do? I'll tell you. I'm going away. By myself. Before it is too late. I'm going tomorrow."

He didn't seem to be taking it in.

"Beattie will come and look after you and the children. She'll be glad to. It won't cost you a penny more than it does now," she added.

He stood staring at her, his flaccid hands hanging down, his face sagging.

"Then you meant what it said in the paper, 'Last Hope'?" he said.

"Yes," she answered.

The Ending

- Talk in your group about your reading of the story and the way it ends, comparing it with your earlier predictions about the ending.
- Make a note of any differences between (a) the endings predicted by group members and (b) the predicted endings and the one written by Marjorie Barnard. Try to suggest why differences may have occurred.
- Share the results of your talk in a whole class discussion.

Whose Prediction?

"The Lottery" is usually described as a feminist text, because it can be argued to support a sympathetic reading of a woman who decides to leave her family. In a study made of how four hundred students read this story, however, most of the readings produced by boys were sympathetic to Ted, while most readings produced by girls were sympathetic to Grace.

The students appeared to read the text in quite different ways, even quoting the *same* parts of the story in support of opposing readings. The following passage, for example, was cited by many boys as support for their reading of Ted as "a good fellow." The girls also referred to this passage, but as evidence of Ted's smugness. They read the phrase, "a good fellow" as Ted's opinion of himself:

> Everyone liked Ted in a kind sort of way. He was a good fellow in both senses of the word. Not namby pamby, always ready for a joke but a good citizen too, a good husband and father. He wasn't the sort that refused to wheel the perambulator. He flourished the perambulator. His wife could hold up her head, they paid their bills weekly and he even put something away, not much but something, and that was a triumph the way things were, the ten per cent knocked off his salary in the depression not restored yet, and one thing and another. And always cheerful, with a joke for everyone. *All this was vaguely present in Ted's mind.* He'd always expected in a trusting sort of way to be rewarded, but not through Grace. (Italics added)

Many of the boys read the following lines as evidence of Ted's generosity, but most girls foregrounded the reference to power and produced other readings:

> They stood mutely by Eric's gate. An idea began to flicker in Ted's mind, and with it came a feeling of sweetness and happiness *and power* such as he had never expected to feel. "I won't see you stuck, old man," he said. (Italics added)

■ In your group, discuss reasons for these differences, in terms of what readings are *available* or *possible* vis-à-vis Grace's decision to leave her family, and in whose interests they might be made.

Dominant versus Resistant Reading?

The boys may have produced a dominant social reading, by condemning Grace for leaving her family. That is, the boys resisted producing the reading apparently invited by the story, a reading that would be *critical* of a dominant social reading.

■ Read the following predictions written by four students ranging from fourteen to seventeen years old.

> I think the story will end with the couple moving out of their old house and into a new more modern home. And they will become closer to each other. Ted will give some of his money to his mate Eric. The reasons for this are that Ted has always been happy and humble, he is always generous.

The story will end in a happy way because Ted is a good fellow and everyone likes him. He deserved the money and he will spend it or use it in a wise way.

I think the story will end with Ted going home to find his wife gone with the money. I feel that Grace had a horrible life staying at home and looking after the children. So I feel the lottery ticket was Grace's last hope to get away from Ted and this unhappy life of hers.

I think that the story will end with Grace not being home. She would have realized that she wasn't reliant on her husband anymore and wished to start again. I think she would have left the children with the husband and along with them, left him a substantial amount of money. Ted would then think about how she really had worked hard and that she made such an effort to get the money because she felt it was her only way out.

■ In your group, discuss how readers can construct such different readings of "The Lottery" and why they might do so. Take notes to report back in a class discussion. You could structure your discussion on the following questions:

a. possible readings of "The Lottery";
b. how these readings might be constructed;
c. what already-available readings might be operating in these readings of the story (for example, you could consider the different ways in which women who leave their families might be thought about at particular times and places);
d. what values are supported by different readings and whose interests are best served by particular readings.

"Looking for a Rain God"

The next story, by Bessie Head, a South African writer who lived in Botswana for much of her life, might be read as offering readers a position from which to reread certain issues. Sometimes readers can take up positions from which they read cultures not their own as bizarre and "primitive." This story, however, might be read as disrupting positions of certainty and superiority for readers.

Looking for a Rain God

Bessie Head

It is lonely at the lands where the people go to plough. These lands are vast clearings in the bush, and the wild bush is lonely too. Nearly all the lands are within walking distance from the village. In some parts of the bush where the underground water is very near the surface, people made little rest camps for themselves and dug shallow wells to quench their thirst while on their journey to their own lands. They experienced all kinds of things once they left the village. They could rest at shady watering places full of lush, tangled trees with delicate pale-gold and purple wild flowers springing up between soft green moss and the children could hunt around for wild figs and any berries that might be in season. But from 1958, a seven-year drought fell upon the land and even the watering places began to look as dismal as the dry open thorn-bush country; the leaves of the trees curled up and withered; the moss became dry and hard and, under the shade of the tangled trees, the ground turned a powdery black and white, because there was no rain. People said rather humorously that if you tried to catch the rain in a cup it would only fill a teaspoon. Towards the beginning of the seventh year of drought, the summer had become an anguish to live through. The air was so dry and moisture-free that it burned the skin. No one knew what to do to escape the heat, and tragedy was in the air. At the beginning of that summer, a number of men just went out of their homes and hung themselves to death from trees. The majority of the people had lived off crops, but for two years past they had all returned from the lands with only their rolled-up skin blankets and cooking utensils. Only the charlatans, incanters, and witch-doctors made a pile of money during this time because people were always turning to them in desperation for little talismans and herbs to rub on the plough for the crops to grow and the rain to fall.

The rains were late that year. They came in early November, with a promise of good rain. It wasn't the full, steady downpour of the years of good rain, but thin, scanty, misty rain. It softened the earth and a rich growth of green things sprang up everywhere for the animals to eat. People were called to the village kgotla (meeting place) to hear the proclamation of the beginning of the ploughing season; they stirred themselves and whole families began to move off to the lands to plough.

The family of the old man, Mokgobja, were among those who left early off the lands. They had a donkey cart and piled everything onto it, Mokgobja who was over seventy years old; two little girls, Neo and Boseyong; their mother Tiro and an unmarried sister, Nesta; and the father and supporter of the family, Ramadi, who drove the donkey cart. In the rush of the first hope of rain, the man, Ramadi and the two women, cleared the land of thorn-bush and then hedged their vast ploughing area with the same thorn-bush to protect the future crop from the goats they had brought along for milk. They cleared out and deepened the old well with its pool of muddy water and still in this light, mist rain, Ramadi inspanned* two oxen and turned the earth over with a hand plough.

The land was ready and ploughed, waiting for the crops. At night, the earth was alive with insects singing and rustling about in search of food. But suddenly, by mid-November, the rain fled away; the rain-clouds fled away and left the sky bare. The sun danced dizzily in the sky, with a strange cruelty. Each day the land was covered in a haze of mist as the sun sucked up the last drop of moisture out of the earth. The family sat down in despair, waiting and waiting. Their hopes had run so high; the goats had started producing milk, which they had eagerly poured on their porridge, now they ate plain porridge with no milk. It was impossible to plant the

* *Inspanned:* yoked.

corn, maize, pumpkin and water-melon seeds in the dry earth. They sat the whole day in the shadow of the huts and even stopped thinking, for the rain had fled away. Only the children, Neo and Boseyong, were quite happy in their little girl world. They carried on with their game of making house like their mother and chattered to each other in light, soft tones. They made children from sticks around which they tied rags, and scolded them severely in an exact imitation of their own mother. Their voices could be heard scolding the day long: "You stupid thing, when I send you to draw water, why do you spill half of it out of the bucket!" "You stupid thing! Can't you mind the porridge-pot without letting the porridge burn!" And then they would beat the rag-dolls on their bottoms with severe expressions.

The adults paid no attention to this; they did not even hear the funny chatter; they sat waiting for rain; their nerves were stretched to breaking-point willing the rain to fall out of the sky. Nothing was important, beyond that. All their animals had been sold during the bad years to purchase food, and of all their herd only two goats were left. It was the women of the family who finally broke down under the strain of waiting for rain. It was really the two women who caused the death of the little girls. Each night they started a weird, high-pitched wailing that began on a low, mournful note and whipped up to a frenzy. Then they would stamp their feet and shout as though they had lost their heads. The men sat quiet and self-controlled; it was important for men to maintain their self-control at all times but their nerve was breaking too. They knew the women were haunted by the starvation of the coming year.

Finally, an ancient memory stirred in the old man, Mokgobja. When he was very young and the customs of the ancestors still ruled the land, he had been witness to a rain-making ceremony. And he came alive a little, struggling to recall the details which had been buried by years and years of prayer in a Christian church. As soon as the mists cleared a little, he began consulting in whispers with his youngest son, Ramadi. There was, he said, a certain rain god who accepted only the sacrifice of the bodies of children. Then the rain would fall; then the crops would grow, he said. He explained the ritual and as he talked, his memory became a conviction and he began to talk with unshakable authority. Ramadi's nerves were smashed by the nightly wailing of the women and soon the two men began whispering with the two women. The children continued their game: "You stupid thing! How could you have lost the money on the way to the shop! You must have been playing again!"

After it was all over and the bodies of the two little girls had been spread across the land, the rain did not fall. Instead, there was a deathly silence at night and the devouring heat of the sun by day. A terror, extreme and deep, overwhelmed the whole family. They packed, rolling up their skin blankets and pots, and fled back to the village.

People in the village soon noted the absence of the two little girls. They had died at the lands and were buried there, the family said. But people noted their ashen, terror-stricken faces and a murmur arose. What had killed the children, they wanted to know? And the family replied that they had just died. And people said amongst themselves that it was strange that the two deaths had occurred at the same time. And there was a feeling of great unease at the unnatural looks of the family. Soon the police came around. The family told them the same story of death and burial at the lands. They did not know what the children had died of. So the police asked to see the graves. At this, the mother of the children broke down and told everything.

Throughout that terrible summer the story of the children hung like a dark cloud of sorrow over the village, and the sorrow was not assuaged when the old man and Ramadi were sentenced to death for ritual murder. All they had on the statute books was that ritual murder was against the law and must be stamped out with the death penalty. The subtle story of strain, starvation and breakdown was inadmissible evidence at court; but all the people who lived off crops knew in their hearts that only a hair's breadth had saved them from sharing a fate similar to that of the Mokgobja family. They could have killed something to make the rain fall.

Against the Law?

All they had on the statute books was that ritual murder was against the law and must be stamped out with the death penalty.

■ With a partner, discuss whether this sentence might be read as:

a. a condemnation of superstition and ignorance;
b. a criticism of the law;
c. a condemnation of ritual murder;
d. support for ritual murder;
e. support for the death penalty;
f. a comment on the inadequacy of the law;
g. support for the law;
h. equating the death penalty with ritual murder;
i. other?

■ Compare readings in your group, before discussing as a class how "Looking for a Rain God" might be read if it ended with the sentence about the death penalty.

Positioning the Reader?

It might be expected that ritual murder would be condemned, but the text appears to position the reader ambiguously. The killing of the children is not condoned, but a position to simply approve of applying the death penalty is not offered. Meanings seem to slip about!

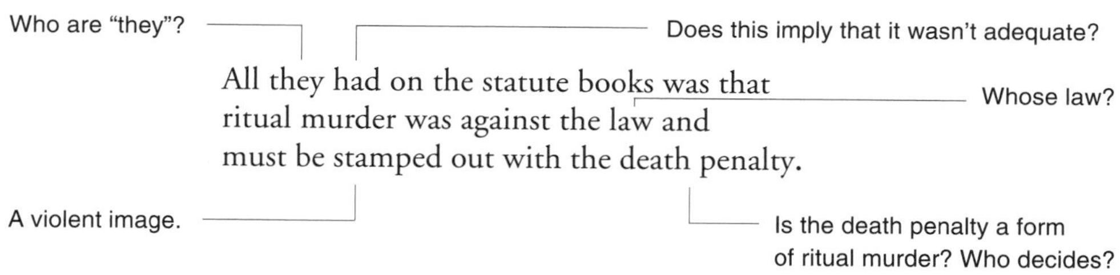

Who are "they"?

Does this imply that it wasn't adequate?

All they had on the statute books was that
ritual murder was against the law and
must be stamped out with the death penalty.

Whose law?

A violent image.

Is the death penalty a form
of ritual murder? Who decides?

A Subtle Story?

> The subtle story of strain and starvation and breakdown was inadmissible evidence at court; but all the people who lived off crops knew in their hearts that only a hair's breadth had saved them from sharing a fate similar to that of the Mokgobja family. They could have killed something to make the rain fall.

How might the ending be read? The use of the word "subtle" might signify a complexity which, it could be argued, readers should not ignore. The characters who might judge—"all the people who lived off crops"—are "placed" ambiguously: "they could have killed something to make the rain fall." A reading can be produced which allows readers to consider how people might want something so badly they could sacrifice or kill for it.

This last paragraph *could* be read as an attempt to disrupt the possibility of readers producing a reading of the Mokgobja family as simply reverting to primitive and superstitious beliefs.

A Rereading?

What it may further allow is a rereading of a *position* that some readers may be tempted to take up. That is, some readers might be tempted to take up a reading position as more "civilized" spectators of an occurrence which could only happen in a "primitive" society, and in which they could not possibly be implicated.

- In your group, discuss possible readings of the last sentences of "Looking for a Rain God," reprinted below with certain words deleted.

  > The subtle story of strain and starvation and breakdown was inadmissible evidence at court; but all the people . . . knew in their hearts that only a hair's breadth had saved them from sharing a fate similar to that of the Mokgobja family. They could have killed something to ____________________.

- Below is a list of substitutions for the last line. Reread the paragraph, making substitutions and discussing possible shifts in the readings produced.

  - ☐ keep peace
  - ☐ stop aggression
  - ☐ prevent the spread of panic
  - ☐ punish the guilty
  - ☐ guarantee oil supplies
  - ☐ protect a nation's sovereignty
  - ☐ prevent war
  - ☐ restore democracy
  - ☐ maintain their living standards
  - ☐ restore economic stability
  - ☐ restore the elected government
  - ☐ end the war

- Discuss the use of the word "something" in the line, "They could have killed something to. . . ." What effect might the substitution of the word "someone" have on the readings produced by readers?

Producing a Rereading

- In your group, read the extract below.

> It was *really* the two women who caused the death of the little girls. Each night they started a weird, high-pitched wailing that began on a low, mournful note and whipped up to a frenzy. Then they would stamp their feet and shout as though they had lost their heads. The men sat quiet and self-controlled; *it was important for men to maintain their self-control at all times* but their nerve was breaking too. (italics added)

- While it would be easy to construct a reading of the women being to blame for the children's death, other readings are possible. In your group, discuss how, for example, you might read the words placed in italics if you were constructing a reading which resists blaming the women.
- Consider, as a class, on what bases readers might choose between a reading that blames the women and one that resists blaming them.

5 Reflecting Life?

This chapter explores ideas about texts and their relationship to "reality" through readings of racism. Texts have been assumed by many critics to reflect or mirror the world. More recently, it has been argued that texts *promote* particular readings of reality, which are never neutral.

"The Test"

Published first in 1940, "The Test," by Angelica Gibbs, has been read in very different ways since then. It has been described as a pleasing example of a storyteller's skills, as a powerful condemnation of racial prejudice, and as a narrative that promotes a particular view of racism that "lets white readers off the hook and is insulting to black readers."

Like the first two readings of "The Test" above, the following critic appears to believe that literature reflects life. It is assumed that there is a meaning in the text which will be obvious to all readers and that words are labels for describing what is "there."

> "The Test" is short, and told largely through dialogue. The characters reveal themselves, and the problems of racial prejudice which the story exposes, through the dialogue. The author never intrudes, and there is almost no exposition. The story offers its insights through the speech of its characters, and is content to let readers observe, for themselves, events as they unfold.

In Whose Interests?

The reading above assumes that "The Test" is *describing* racism and condemning it. Another argument is that (a) "The Test" supports a reading of racism in certain terms, and (b) those terms serve the interests of black and white readers quite differently. The following readings are representative of these positions.

> a. The reading of "The Test" as a condemnation of racism has been argued to support white readers because they can distance themselves from the inspector, who is read as the only racist in the story. Racism then can be read as the actions of bad white people. The white reader can take up an apparently nonracist position by condemning the inspector for his actions.

b. The reading of "The Test" as a condemnation of racism does not challenge the ways in which exploitation of black people is justified in the story. Marian, the black woman in the story, is constructed as apparently enjoying an affectionate relationship with her white employer, Mrs. Ericson. Mrs. Ericson can be read as being involved in racial exploitation, through her role as an employer of a black woman as a servant. The apparently friendly relationship she has with Marian merely disguises this less explicit form of oppression.

■ Consider these arguments as you read "The Test."

The Test

Angelica Gibbs

On the afternoon Marian took her second driver's test, Mrs. Ericson went with her.

"It's probably better to have someone a little older with you," Mrs. Ericson said as Marian slipped into the driver's seat beside her. "Perhaps the last time your Cousin Bill made you nervous, talking too much on the way."

"Yes, Ma'am," Marian said in her soft unaccented voice. "They probably do like it better if a white person shows up with you."

"Oh, I don't think it's *that*," Mrs. Ericson began, and subsided after a glance at the girl's set profile. Marian drove the car slowly through the shady suburban streets. It was one of the first hot days in June, and when they reached the boulevard they found it crowded with cars headed for the beaches.

"Do you want me to drive?" Mrs. Ericson asked. "I'll be glad to if you're feeling jumpy." Marian shook her head. Mrs. Ericson watched her dark, competent hands and wondered for the thousandth time how the house had ever managed to get along without her, or how she had lived through those earlier years when her household had been presided over by a series of slatternly white girls who had considered housework demeaning and the care of children an added insult. "You drive beautifully, Marian," she said. "Now, don't think of the last time. Anybody would slide on a steep hill on a wet day like that."

"It takes four mistakes to flunk you," Marian said. "I don't remember doing all the things the inspector marked down on my blank."

"People say that they only want you to slip them a little something," Mrs. Ericson said doubtfully.

"*No*," Marian said. "That would only make it worse, Mrs. Ericson, I know."

The car turned right, at a traffic signal, into a side road and slid up to the curb at the rear of a short line of parked cars. The inspector had not arrived yet.

"You have the papers?" Mrs. Ericson asked. Marian took them out of her bag: her learner's permit, the car registration, and her birth certificate. They settled down to the dreary business of waiting.

"It will be marvellous to have someone dependable to drive the children to school every day," Mrs. Ericson said. Marian looked up from the list of driving requirements she had been studying. "It will make things simpler at the house, won't it?" she said.

"Oh, Marian," Mrs. Ericson exclaimed, "if I could only pay you half of what you're worth!"

"Now, Mrs. Ericson," Marian said firmly. They looked at each other and smiled with affection.

Two cars with official insignia on their doors stopped across the street. The inspectors leaped out, very brisk and military in their neat uniforms. Marian's hands tightened on the wheel. "There's the one who flunked me last time," she whispered, pointing to a stocky, self-important man who had begun to shout directions at the driver at the head of the line. "Oh, Mrs. Ericson."

"Now Marian," Mrs. Ericson said. They smiled at each other again, rather weakly.

The inspector who finally reached their car was not the stocky one but a genial, middle-aged man who grinned broadly as he thumbed over their papers. Mrs. Ericson started to get out of the car. "Don't you want to come along?" the inspector asked. "Mandy and I don't mind company."

Mrs. Ericson was bewildered for a moment. "No," she said, and stepped to the curb. "I might make Marian self-conscious. She's a fine driver, Inspector."

"Sure thing," the inspector said, winking at Mrs. Ericson. He slid into the seat beside Marian. "Turn right at the corner, Mandy-Lou."

From the curb, Mrs. Ericson watched the car move smoothly up the street. The inspector made notations in a small black book. "Age?" he inquired presently, as they drove along.

"Twenty-seven."

He looked at Marian out of the corner of his eye. "Old enough to have quite a flock of pickaninnies, eh?"

Marian did not answer.

"Left at this corner," the inspector said, "and park between that truck and the green Buick."

The two cars were very close together, but Marian squeezed in between them without too much manoeuvring. "Driven before, Mandy-Lou?" the inspector asked.

"Yes, sir. I had a licence for three years in Pennsylvania."

"Why do you want to drive a car?"

"My employer needs me to take her children to and from school."

"Sure you don't really want to sneak out nights to meet some young blood?" the inspector asked. He laughed as Marian shook her head.

"Let's see you take a left at the corner and then turn around in the middle of the next block," the inspector said. He began to whistle *Swanee River*. "Make you homesick?" he asked.

Marian put out her hand, swung around neatly in the street, and headed back in the direction from which they had come. "No," she said. "I was born in Scranton, Pennsylvania."

The inspector feigned astonishment. "You-all ain't Southern?" he said. "Well, dog my cats if I didn't think you-all came from down yonder."

"No, sir," Marian said.

"Turn onto Main Street and let's see how you-all does in heavier traffic."

They followed a line of cars along Main Street for several blocks until they came in sight of a concrete bridge which arched high over the railroad tracks.

"Read that sign at the end of the bridge," the inspector said.

"Proceed with caution. Dangerous in slippery weather," Marian said.

"You-all sho can read fine," the inspector exclaimed. "Where d'you learn to do that, Mandy?"

"I got my college degree last year," Marian said. Her voice was not quite steady.

As the car crept up the slope of the bridge the inspector burst out laughing. He laughed so hard he could scarcely give his next direction.

"Stop here," he said, wiping his eyes, "Then start 'er up again. Mandy got her degree, did she? Dog my cats!"

Marian pulled up beside the curb. She put the car into gear again. Her face was set. As she released the brake her foot slipped off the clutch pedal and the engine stalled.

"Now, Mistress Mandy," the inspector said, "remember your degree."

"*Damn* you!" Marian cried. She started the car with a jerk.

The inspector lost his joviality in an instant. "Return to the starting place, please," he said, and made four very black crosses at random in the squares on Marian's application blank.

Mrs. Ericson was waiting at the curb where they had left her. As Marian stopped the car, the inspector jumped out and brushed past her, his face purple. "What happened?" Mrs. Ericson asked, looking at him with alarm.

Marian stared down at the wheel and her lip trembled.

"Oh, Marian, *again*?" Mrs. Ericson said.

Marian nodded. "In a sort of different way," she said, and slid over to the right-hand side of the car.

- Having read the story, reread and discuss in your group the arguments presented before the story, and then work through the following activities.

What Might Be Read as Racist or the Result of Racism?

It might be argued that readers are positioned by "The Test" to read some actions or events as racist and not others.

- With a partner, discuss each of the following statements and complete them (1) as you think "The Test" encourages you to read them and (2) in alternative ways:

  a. The inspector fails Marian because she is a poor driver / is black / is over-emotional / is a woman / curses him.
  b. The inspector fails Marian because he is racist / is sexist / has no choice / is upset.
  c. Marian, a college graduate, works as a home helper because she is black / is unskilled / is skilled / chooses to / has no choice.
  d. Marian is paid less than half of what she is worth because she is black / is a woman / it's the going rate.
  e. Mrs. Ericson employs Marian because she is kind / is racist / has no choice / prefers college graduates.

Gaps and Naming

Texts are always fragmentary. Particular ways of reading, or reading practices, work to fill gaps so that readers are unaware of them. This is because gaps are often filled with taken-for-granted ways of thinking.

- In your group, discuss why the text doesn't "tell" readers:

  a. why Mrs. Ericson has household help;
  b. what academic qualifications Mrs. Ericson has;
  c. whether Mrs. Ericson has an unaccented voice;
  d. why Marian works as a housekeeper;
  e. what race the inspector is.

Naming—who calls whom what, and why—is usually not thought about explicitly, but attention is drawn to it in "The Test."

- In your group, complete the following:

  a. Marian calls the inspector "Sir" because . . .
  b. The inspector calls Marian "Mandy Lou" because . . .
  c. Marian calls her employer "Mrs. Ericson" because . . .
  d. Mrs. Ericson calls Marian "Marian" because . . .
  e. The inspector is not named in "The Test" because . . .
  f. Marian is not given a second name in "The Test" because . . .

"A Way of Talking"

When you reach the middle of the next page of Patricia Grace's short story, "A Way of Talking," pause for a few minutes and, with a partner, discuss what type of story you think it is, and what you think might follow.

A Way of Talking

Patricia Grace

Rose came back yesterday; we went down to the bus to meet her. She's just the same as ever Rose. Talks all the time flat out and makes us laugh with her way of talking. On the way home we kept saying, "E Rohe,[1] you're just the same as ever." It's good having my sister back and knowing she hasn't changed. Rose is the hard-case one in the family, the kama-kama one, and the one with the brains. Last night we stayed up talking till all hours, even Dad and Nanny who usually go to bed after tea. Rose made us laugh telling about the people she knows, and taking off professor this and professor that from varsity. Nanny, Mum, and I had tears running down from laughing; e ta Rose we laughed all night.

At last Nanny got out of her chair and said, "Time for sleeping. The mouths steal the time of the eyes." That's the lovely way she has of talking, Nanny, when she speaks in English. So we went to bed and Rose and I kept our mouths going for another hour or so before falling asleep.

This morning I said to Rose that we'd better go and get her measured for the dress up at Mrs. Frazer's. Rose wanted to wait a day or two but I reminded her the wedding was only two weeks away and that Mrs. Frazer had three frocks to finish.

"Who's Mrs. Frazer anyway?" she asked. Then I remembered Rose hadn't met these neighbours though they'd been in the district a few years. Rose had been away at school.

"She's a dressmaker." I looked for words. "She's nice."

"What sort of nice?"

"Rose, don't you say anything funny when we go up there," I said. I know Rose, she's smart. "Don't you get smart." I'm older than Rose but she's the one that speaks out when something doesn't please her. Mum used to say, Rohe you've got the brains but you look to your sister for the sense. I started to feel funny about taking Rose up to Jane Frazer's because Jane often says the wrong thing without knowing.

We got our work done, had a bath and changed, and when Dad came back from the shed we took the station wagon to drive over to Jane's. Before we left we called out to Mum, "Don't forget to make us a Maori bread for when we get back."

"What's wrong with your own hands," Mum said, but she was only joking. Always when one of us comes home one of the first things she does is make a big Maori bread.

---

1. *E* functions here similarly to *hey,* and *Rohe* is a nickname for *Rose. Kama-kama* means "full of spirits." *Varsity* indicates *university. E ta* is akin to *man* as in a salutation or greeting.

Rose made a good impression with her kama-kama ways, and Jane's two nuisance kids took a liking to her straight away. They kept jumping up and down on the sofa to get Rose's attention and I kept thinking what a waste of a good sofa it was, what a waste of a good house for those two nuisance things. I hope when I have kids they won't be so hoha.[2]

I was pleased about Jane and Rose. Jane was asking Rose all sorts of questions about her life in Auckland. About varsity and did Rose join in the marches and demonstrations. Then they went on to talking about fashions and social life in the city, and Jane seemed deeply interested. Almost as though she was jealous of Rose and the way she lived, as though she felt Rose had something better than a lovely old house and clothes and everything she needed to make life good for her. I was pleased to see that Jane liked my sister so much, and proud of my sister and her entertaining and friendly ways.

Jane made a cup of coffee when she'd finished measuring Rose for the frock, then packed the two kids outside with a piece of chocolate cake each. We were sitting having coffee when we heard a truck turn in at the bottom of Frazer's drive.

Jane said, "That's Alan. He's been down the road getting the Maoris for scrub cutting."

What Next?

Pause here to discuss, with a partner, what type of story you think "A Way of Talking" is, and where you think it might go from here. The story continues:

I felt my face get hot. I was angry. At the same time I was hoping Rose would let the remark pass. I tried hard to think of something to say to cover Jane's words though I'd hardly said a thing all morning. But my tongue seemed to thicken and all I could think of was Rohe don't.

Rose was calm. Not all red and flustered like me. She took a big pull on the cigarette she had lit, squinted her eyes up and blew the smoke out gently. I knew something was coming.

"Don't they have names?"

"What. Who?" Jane was surprised and her face was getting pink.

"The people from down the road whom your husband is employing to cut scrub." Rose the stink thing, she was talking all Pakehafied.[3]

"I don't know any of their names."

I was glaring at Rose because I wanted her to stop but she was avoiding my looks and pretending to concentrate on her cigarette.

---

2. *Hoha:* wearisome.

3. *Pakeha* refers to a person who is not of Maori descent, or a white person. As suggested later in the story, the connotation may vary.

"Do they know yours?"

"Mine?"

"Your name."

"Well . . . Yes."

"Yet you have never bothered to find out their names or to wonder whether or not they have any."

The silence seemed to bang around in my head for ages and ages. Then I think Jane muttered something about difficulty, but that touchy sister of mine stood up and said, "Come on Hera." And I with my red face and shut mouth followed her out to the station wagon without a goodbye or anything.

I was so wild with Rose. I was wild. I was determined to blow her up about what she had done, I was determined. But now that we were alone together I couldn't think what to say. Instead, I felt an awful big sulk coming on. It has always been my trouble, sulking. Whenever I don't feel sure about something I go into a big fat sulk. We had a teacher at school who used to say to some of us girls, "Speak, don't sulk." She'd say, "You only sulk because you haven't learned how and when to say your minds."

She was right that teacher, yet here I am a young woman about to be married and haven't learned yet how to get the words out. Dad used to say to me, "Look out girlie, you'll stand on your lip."

At last I said, "Rose, you're a stink thing." Tears were on the way. "Gee Rohe, you made me embarrassed."

Then Rose said, "Don't worry, Honey, she's got a thick hide."

These words of Rose's took me by surprise and I realised something about Rose then. What she said made all my anger go away and I felt very sad because it's not our way of talking to each other. Usually we'd say, "Never mind Sis," if we wanted something to be forgotten. But when Rose said, "Don't worry Honey she's got a thick hide," it made her seem a lot older than me, and tougher, and as though she knew much more than me about the world. It made me realise too that underneath her jolly and forthright ways Rose is very hurt. I remembered back to when we were both little and Rose used to play up at school if she didn't like the teacher. She'd get smart and I used to be ashamed and tell Mum on her when we got home, because although she had the brains I was always the well behaved one.

Rose was speaking to me in a new way now. It made me feel sorry for her and for myself. All my life I had been sitting back and letting her do the objecting. Not only me, but Mum and Dad and the rest of the family too. All of us too scared to make known when we had been hurt or slighted. And how can the likes of Jane know when we go round pretending all is well. How can Jane know us?

But then I tried to put another thought into words. I said to Rose, "We do it too. We say 'the Pakeha doctor,' or 'the Pakeha at the post office,' and sometimes we mean it in a bad way."

"Except that we talk like this to each other only. It's not so much what is said, but when and where and in whose presence. Besides, you and I don't speak in this way now, not since we were little. It's the older ones: Mum, Dad, Nanny who have this habit."

Then Rose said something else. "Jane Frazer will still want to be your friend and mine in spite of my embarrassing her today; we're in the fashion."

"What do you mean?"

"It's fashionable for a Pakeha to have a Maori for a friend." Suddenly Rose grinned. Then I heard Jane's voice coming out of Rohe's mouth and felt a grin of my own coming. "I have friends who are Maoris. They're lovely people. The eldest girl was married recently and I did the frocks. The other girl is at varsity. They're all so *friendly* and so *natural* and their house is absolutely *spotless.*"

I stopped the wagon in the drive and when we'd got out Rose started strutting up the path. I saw Jane's way of walking and felt a giggle coming on. Rose walked up Mum's scrubbed steps, "Absolutely spotless." She left her shoes in the porch and bounced into the kitchen. "What did I tell you? Absolutely spotless. And a friendly natural woman taking new bread from the oven."

Mum looked at Rose then at me. "What have you two been up to? Rohe I hope you behaved yourself at that Pakeha place?" But Rose was setting the table. At the sight of Mum's bread she'd forgotten all about Jane and the events of the morning.

When Dad, Heke, and Matiu came in for lunch, Rose, Mum, Nanny and I were already into the bread and the big bowl of hot corn.

"E ta," Dad said. "Let your hardworking father and your two hardworking brothers starve. Eat up."

"The bread's terrible. You men better go down to the shop and get you a shop bread," said Rose.

"Be the day," said Heke.

"Come on my fat Rohe. Move over and make room for your Daddy. Come on my baby shift over."

Dad squeezed himself round behind the table next to Rose. He picked up the bread Rose had buttered for herself and started eating. "The bread's terrible all right," he said. Then Mat and Heke started going on about how awful the corn was and who cooked it and who grew it, who watered it all summer and who pulled out the weeds.

So I joined in the carryings on and forgot about Rose and Jane for the meantime. But I'm not leaving it at that. I'll find some way of letting Rose know I understand and I know it will be difficult for me because I'm not clever the way she is. I can't say things the same and I've never learnt to stick up for myself.

But my sister won't have to be alone again. I'll let her know that.

Rereading Racism?

"A Way of Talking" seems to promote a reading of the lines, "That's Alan. He's been down the road getting the Maoris for scrub cutting," as racist.

Jane, the character who speaks these lines, might be read as unwittingly offensive to Rose and her sister. Unlike the character of the inspector in "The Test," Jane is not constructed as intentionally offending, but as doing so nevertheless.

Racism appears to be constructed here not simply as the individual actions of a person, but as a "way of talking." That is, the language available to a specific character as a member of a particular group—the language that may seem most natural and normal in a white culture—is viewed here as racist.

The racism, however, doesn't exist "in" the line. Substituting other words in place of "The Maoris" can produce shifts in readings. For example, if the reference is to "The Australians" or "The English" or "The doctors," the readings might change depending on who was making the reading and under what conditions. It also seems to depend on the *already available* readings of the group mentioned.

In complex ways, social power relations, which are often unequal and unjust, are systematically maintained and reproduced in everyday language use—in ways of talking.

"A Way of Talking" might be read as a story that is promoting a reading of racism that is rather more complex than that of "The Test." Racism is presented as something white readers may not "mean." Nevertheless, it can be argued that "A Way of Talking" promotes a reading of racism as being a part of white language and culture.

Comparing "A Way of Talking" with "The Test"

Texts may present characters in ways that appear to invite a sympathetic reading and yet by which they are largely marginalized or silenced. One way of trying to consider the different ways in which characters might be constructed is to compare them in terms of the following questions.

- In your pair, copy the chart on the next page and then complete it by checking the column or columns that you would argue are appropriate. This should help you to consider different readings.
- Compare your decisions in your group, making any changes that you are persuaded to, before reporting back to the class.

	"The Test"			"A Way of Talking"		
Characters	Marian	Mrs. Ericson	Inspector	Rose	Narrator	Jane
Who speaks?						
Who listens?						
Who is active?						
Who is passive?						
Who is powerful?						
Who is powerless?						
Who is rational?						
Who is emotional?						

For Class Discussion

1. In what ways might the relationships between the three characters in each story be read?
2. How might Mrs. Ericson and Jane be read as similar characters?
3. In what ways do the texts appear to promote very different readings of Mrs. Ericson and Jane?
4. How might the actions of Marian in "The Test" and Rose and her sister in "A Way of Talking" be read in similar *and* different ways?

Readers, Readings, and Texts

In the study of students' readings of "The Lottery," described earlier, it was claimed that the majority of girls and the majority of boys read that story in quite different and opposing ways. In a parallel way, it has been suggested that many readers of different races might read "The Test" and "A Way of Talking" differently. Consider, for example, the following:

> "The Test" has been described as "a 'feeling good about feeling bad' story for white readers." That is, white readers can feel sad or bad about what has happened to Marian and know that they are not racist like the inspector—and so feel good. For black readers, however, this reading of "The Test" has been called insulting in that Marian is first shown as grateful to Mrs. Ericson, and then when she speaks out against the inspector she is silenced.
>
> "A Way of Talking" has been called an "empowering story for black readers" who can read the black characters as strong and certainly not silenced. It has been termed "an uncomfortable read" for white readers since it seems to be suggesting that white racism often may be unintentional, and that quite ordinary people—all whites?—might be guilty of it and need to "unlearn" it.

1. In what ways do you think readers of different races might be positioned differently by "The Test" and "A Way of Talking"?
2. In what ways do you think readers of different races might be positioned differently by the two arguments (above) about readings of "The Test" and "A Way of Talking"?
3. What else may position readers in considering these readings? For example, how might a reader's gender, education, history, class, religion, or politics play a part in the readings she or he produces?

6 Real People?

It is possible to read the following two stories as if they are reflections of "true to life situations" in which a teenage boy and a teenage girl, respectively, are confronted with decisions about their futures.

If characters are considered to be "true to life" or like "real people," readers generally try to explain the characters' behavior in terms of the sorts of things people might do in real-life situations. The problem with this approach is that it does not allow readers to explain their readings of why characters might do one thing or another, other than to say it's because that's what they are "like." This becomes a circular argument in which it is claimed that a character does something because that's what the character is like, and the character is like this because of what he or she does.

In trying to decide what a character is like, readers often assign different meanings to the same behavior or actions of characters. These meanings, this book argues, are not reflections of what the character is "like" but are produced out of already available readings of how characters (of a particular gender, race, or social class) might, or should, behave.

To view characters as "real people" is part of a relatively modern reading practice, which assumes characters' meanings lie "within them." By focusing on what a particular character is "like," questions tend not to be asked about how and why characters are read in particular ways.

"Manhood"

■ Before reading the story which follows, discuss these questions in your group, taking notes on your decisions:

1. What do you think a story called "Manhood," from which the following extract is taken, could be about?

   There is a law. The unalterable law of nature that says that the young males of the species indulge in manly trials of strength. Think of all the other lads who are going into the ring tonight. D'you think their mothers are sitting about crying and kicking up a fuss? No—they're proud to have strong, masculine sons who can stand up in the ring and take a few punches.

2. What might be other readings of the term "manhood"?

3. Is there a female equivalent to "manhood"? What does the word "womanhood" suggest to you? Are girls expected to *prove* themselves before they can become young women?

■ Share your answers in a class discussion. Then, individually, write a paragraph beginning, "There is a law. The unalterable law of nature that says that the young females of the species . . ."

Manhood

John Wain

Swiftly free-wheeling, their breath coming easily, the man and the boy steered their bicycles down the short dip which led them from woodland into open country. Then they looked ahead and saw that the road began to climb.

"Now Rob," said Mr. Willison, settling his plump haunches firmly on the saddle, just up that rise and we'll get off and have a good rest."

"Can't we rest now?" the boy asked. "My legs feel all funny. As if they're turning to water."

"Rest at the top," said Mr. Willison firmly. "Remember what I told you? The first thing any athlete has to learn is to break the fatigue barrier."

"I've broken it already. I was feeling tired when we were going along the main road and I—"

"When fatigue sets in, the thing to do is to keep going until it wears off. Then you get your second wind and your second endurance."

"I've already done that."

"Up we go," said Mr. Willison, "and at the top we'll have a good rest." He panted slightly and stood on his pedals, causing his machine to sway from side to side in a laboured manner. Rob, falling silent, pushed doggedly at his pedals. Slowly, the pair wavered up the straight road to the top. Once there, Mr. Willison dismounted with exaggerated steadiness, laid his bicycle carefully on its side, and spread his jacket on the ground before sinking down to rest. Rob slid hastily from the saddle and flung himself full-length on the grass.

"Don't lie there," said his father. "You'll catch cold."

"I'm all right. I'm warm."

"Come and sit on this. When you're over-heated, that's just when you're prone to—"

"I'm all *right*, Dad. I want to lie here. My back aches."

"Your back needs strengthening, that's why it aches. It's a pity we don't live near a river where you could get some rowing."

The boy did not answer, and Mr. Willison, aware that he was beginning to sound like a nagging, over-anxious parent, allowed himself to be defeated and did not press the suggestion about Rob's coming to sit on his jacket. Instead, he waited a moment and then glanced at his watch.

"Twenty to twelve. We must get going in a minute."

"*What?* I thought we were going to have a rest."

"Well, we're having one, aren't we?" said Mr. Willison reasonably. "I've got my breath back, so surely you must have."

"My back still aches. I want to lie here a bit."

"Sorry," said Mr. Willison, getting up and moving over to his bicycle. "We've got at least twelve miles to do and lunch is at one."

"Dad, why did we have to come so far if we've got to get back for one o'clock? I know, let's find a telephone box and ring up Mum and tell her we—"

"Nothing doing. There's no reason why two fit men shouldn't cycle twelve miles in an hour and ten minutes."

"But we've already done about a million miles."

"We've done about fourteen, by my estimation," said Mr. Willison stiffly. "What's the good of going for a bike ride if you don't cover a bit of distance?"

He picked up his bicycle and stood waiting. Rob, with his hand over his eyes, lay motionless on the grass. His legs looked thin and white among the rich grass.

"Come on, Rob."

The boy showed no sign of having heard. Mr. Willison got on to his bicycle and began to ride slowly away. "Rob," he called over his shoulder, "I'm going."

Rob lay like a sullen corpse by the roadside. He looked horribly like the victim of an accident, unmarked but dead from internal injuries. Mr. Willison cycled fifty yards, then a hundred, then turned in a short, irritable circle and came back to where his son lay.

"Rob, is there something the matter or are you just being awkward?"

The boy removed his hand and looked up into his father's face. His eyes were surprisingly mild: there was no fire or rebellion in them.

"I'm tired and my back aches. I can't go on yet."

"Look, Rob," said Mr. Willison gently. "I wasn't going to tell you this, because I meant it to be a surprise, but when you get home you'll find a present waiting for you."

"What kind of present?"

"Something very special I've bought for you. The man's coming this morning to fix it up. That's one reason why I suggested a bike ride this morning. He'll have done it by now."

"What is it?"

"Aha. It's a surprise. Come on, get on your bike and let's go home and see."

Rob sat up, then slowly clambered to his feet. "Isn't there a short cut home?"

"I'm afraid not. It's only twelve miles."

Rob said nothing.

"And a lot of that's downhill," Mr. Willison added brightly. His own legs were tired and his muscles fluttered unpleasantly. In addition, he suddenly realised he was very thirsty. Rob, still without speaking, picked up his bicycle, and they pedalled away.

"Where is he?" Mrs. Willison asked, coming into the garage.

"Gone up to his room," said Mr. Willison. He doubled his fist and gave the punch-ball a thudding blow. "Seems to have fixed it pretty firmly. You gave him the instructions, I suppose."

"What's he doing up in his room? It's lunch-time."

"He said he wanted to rest a bit."

"I hope you're satisfied," said Mrs. Willison. "A lad of thirteen, nearly fourteen years of age, just when he should have a really big appetite, and when the lunch is put on the table he's *resting*—"

"Now look, I know what I'm—"

"Lying down in his room, resting, too tired to eat because you've dragged him up hill and down dale on one of your—"

"We did nothing that couldn't be reasonably expected of a boy of his age."

"How do you know?" Mrs. Willison demanded. "You never did anything of that kind when you were a boy. How do you know what can be reasonably—"

"Now look," said Mr. Willison again. "When I was a boy, it was study, study, study all the time, with the fear of unemployment and insecurity in everybody's mind. I was never even given a bicycle. I never boxed, I never rowed, I never did anything to develop my physique. It was just work, work, work, pass this exam, get that certificate. Well, I did it and now I'm qualified and in a secure job. But you know as well as I do that they let me down. Nobody encouraged me to build myself up."

"Well, what does it matter? You're all right—"

"Grace!" Mr. Willison interrupted sharply. "I am not all right and you know it. I am under average height, my chest is flat and I'm—"

"What nonsense. You're taller than I am and I'm—"

"No son of mine is going to grow up with the same wretched physical heritage that I—"

"No, he'll just have heart disease through overtaxing his strength, because you haven't got the common sense to—"

"His heart is one hundred per cent all right. Not three weeks have gone by since the doctor looked at him."

"Well, why does he get so over-tired if he's all right? Why is he lying down now instead of coming to the table, a boy of his age?"

A slender shadow blocked part of the dazzling sun in the doorway. Looking up simultaneously, the Willisons greeted their son.

"Lunch ready, Mum? I'm hungry."

"Ready when you are," Grace Willison beamed. "Just wash your hands and come to the table."

"Look Rob," said Mr. Willison. "If you hit it with your left hand and then catch it on the rebound with your right, it's excellent ring training." He dealt the punch-ball two amateurish blows. "That's what they call a right cross," he said.

"I think it's fine. I'll have some fun with it," said Rob. He watched mildly as his father peeled off the padded mittens.

"Here, slip these on," said Mr. Willison. "They're just training gloves. They harden your fists. Of course, we can get a pair of proper gloves later. But these are specially for use with the ball."

"Lunch," called Mrs. Willison from the house.

"Take a punch at it," Mr. Willison urged.

"Let's go and eat."

"Go on. One punch before you go in. I haven't seen you hit it yet."

Rob took the gloves, put on the right-hand one, and gave the punch-ball one conscientious blow, aiming at the exact centre.

"Now let's go in," he said.

"Lunch!"

"All right. We're coming . . ."

"Five feet eight, Rob," said Mr. Willison, folding up the wooden ruler. "You're taller than I am. This is a great landmark."

"Only *just* taller."

"But you're growing all the time. Now all you have to do is to start growing outwards as well as upwards. We'll have you in the middle of that scrum. The heaviest forward in the pack."

Rob picked up his shirt and began uncertainly poking his arms into the sleeves.

"When do they pick the team?" Mr. Willison asked. "I should have thought they'd have done it by now."

"They have done it," said Rob. He bent down to pick up his socks from under a chair.

"They have? And you—"

"I wasn't selected," said the boy, looking intently at the socks as if trying to detect minute differences in colour and weave.

Mr. Willison opened his mouth, closed it again, and stood for a moment looking out of the window. Then he gently laid his hand on his son's shoulder. "Bad luck," he said quietly.

"I tried hard," said Rob quickly.

"I'm sure you did."

"I played my hardest in the trial games."

"It's just bad luck," said Mr. Willison. "It could happen to anybody."

There was silence as they both continued with their dressing. A faint smell of frying rose into the air, and they could hear Mrs. Willison laying the table for breakfast.

"That's it, then, for this season," said Mr. Willison, as if to himself.

"I forgot to tell you, though," said Rob. "I was selected for the boxing team."

"You *were* ? I didn't know the school had one."

"It's new. Just formed. They had some trials for it at the end of last term. I found my punching was better than most people's because I'd been getting plenty of practice with the ball."

Mr. Willison put out a hand and felt Rob's biceps. "Not bad, not bad at all," he said critically. But if you're going to be a boxer and represent the school, you'll need more power up there. I tell you what. We'll train together."

"That'll be fun," said Rob. "I'm training at school too."

"What weight do they put you in?"

"It isn't weight, it's age. Under fifteen. Then when you get over fifteen you get classified into weights."

"Well," said Mr. Willison, tying his tie, "you'll be in a good position for the under-fifteens. You've got six months to play with. And there's no reason why you shouldn't steadily put muscle on all the time. I suppose you'll be entered as a team, for tournaments and things?"

"Yes, there's a big one at the end of next term. I'll be in that."

Confident, joking, they went down to breakfast. "Two eggs for Rob, Mum," said Mr. Willison.

"He's in training. He's going to be a heavyweight."

"A heavyweight what?" Mrs. Willison asked, teapot in hand.

"Boxer," Rob smiled.

Grace Willison put down the teapot, her lips compressed, and looked from one to the other. "*Boxing?*" she repeated.

"Boxing," Mr. Willison replied calmly.

"Over my dead body," said Mrs. Willison. "That's one sport I'm definite that he's never going in for."

"Too late. They've picked him for the under-fifteens. He's had trials and everything."

"Is this true, Rob?" she demanded.

"Yes," said the boy, eating rapidly.

"Well, you can just tell them you're dropping it. Baroness Summerskill—"

"To hell with Baroness Summerskill!" her husband shouted. "The first time he gets a chance to do something, the first time he gets picked for a team and given a chance to show what he's made of, and you have to bring up Baroness Summerskill."

"But it injures their brains! All those blows on the front of the skull. I've read about it—"

"Injures their brains!" Mr. Willison snorted. "Has it injured Ingemar Johansson's brain? Why, he's one of the acutest business men in the world!"

"Rob," said Mrs. Willison steadily, "when you get to school, go and see the sports master and tell him you're giving up boxing."

"There isn't a sports master. All the masters do bits of it at different times."

"There must be one who's in charge of boxing. All you have to do is tell him—"

"Are you ready, Rob?" said Mr. Willison. "You'll be late for school if you don't go."

"I'm in plenty of time, Dad. I haven't finished my breakfast."

"Never mind, push along, old son. You've had your egg and bacon, that's what matters. I want to talk to your mother."

Cramming a piece of dry toast into his mouth, the boy picked up his satchel and wandered from the room. Husband and wife sat back, glaring hot-eyed at each other.

The quarrel began, and continued for many days. In the end it was decided that Rob should continue boxing until he had represented the school at the tournament in March of the following year, and should then give it up.

"Ninety-six, ninety-seven, ninety-eight, ninety-nine, a hundred," Mr. Willison counted. "Right, that's it. Now go and take your shower and get into bed."

"I don't feel tired, honestly," Rob protested.

"Who's manager here, you or me?" Mr. Willison asked bluffly. "I'm in charge of training and you can't say my methods don't work. Fifteen solid weeks and you start questioning my decisions on the very night of the fight?"

"It just seems silly to go to bed when . . ."

"My dear Rob, please trust me. No boxer ever went into a big fight without spending an hour or two in bed, resting before going to his dressing-room."

"All right. But I bet none of the others are bothering to do all this."

"That's exactly why you're going to be better than the others. Now go and get your shower before you catch cold. Leave the skipping rope, I'll put it away."

After Rob had gone, Mr. Willison folded the skipping rope into a neat ball and packed it away in the case that contained the boy's gloves, silk dressing gown, lace-up boxing boots, and trunks with the school badge sewn into the correct position on the right leg. There would be no harm in a little skipping, to limber up and conquer his nervousness while waiting to go on. Humming, he snapped down the catches of the small leather case and went into the house.

Mrs. Willison did not lift her eyes from the television set as he entered. "All ready now, Mother," said Mr. Willison. "He's going to rest in bed now, and go along at about six o'clock. I'll go with him and wait till the doors open to be sure of a ring-side seat." He sat down on the sofa beside his wife, and tried to put his arm round her. "Come on, love," he said coaxingly. "Don't spoil my big night."

She turned to him and he was startled to see her eyes brimming with angry tears. "What about my big night?" she asked, her voice harsh. "Fourteen years ago, remember? When he came into the world."

"Well, what about it?" Mr. Willison parried, uneasily aware that the television set was quacking and signalling on the fringe of his attention, turning the scene from clumsy tragedy into a clumsier farce.

"Why didn't you tell me then?" she sobbed. "Why did you let me have a son if all you were interested in was having him punched to death by a lot of rough bullet-headed louts who—"

"Take a grip on yourself, Grace. A punch on the nose won't hurt him."

"You're an unnatural father," she keened. "I don't know how you can bear to send him into that ring to be beaten and thumped—Oh, why can't you stop him now? Keep him at home? There's no *law* that compels us to—"

"That's where you're wrong, Grace," said Mr. Willison sternly. "There is a law. The unalterable law of nature that says that the young males of the species indulge in manly trials of strength. Think of all the other lads who are going into the ring tonight. D'you think their mothers are sitting about crying and kicking up a fuss? No—they're proud to have strong, masculine sons who can stand up in the ring and take a few punches."

"Go away, please," said Mrs. Willison, sinking back with closed eyes. "Just go right away and don't come near me until it's all over."

"Grace!"

"Please. Please leave me alone. I can't bear to look at you and I can't bear to hear you."

"You're hysterical!" said Mr. Willison bitterly. Rising, he went out into the hall and called up the stairs. "Are you in bed, Rob?"

There was a slight pause and then Rob's voice called faintly, "Could you come up, Dad?"

"Come up? Why? Is something the matter?"

"Could you come up?"

Mr. Willison ran up the stairs. "What is it?" he panted. "D'you want something?"

"I think I've got appendicitis," said Rob. He lay squinting among the pillows, his face suddenly narrow and crafty.

"I don't believe you," said Mr. Willison shortly. "I've supervised your training for fifteen weeks and I know you're as fit as a fiddle. You can't possibly have anything wrong with you."

"I've got a terrible pain in my side," said Rob. "Low down on the right-hand side. That's where appendicitis comes, isn't it?"

Mr. Willison sat down on the bed. "Listen, Rob," he said. "Don't do this to me. All I'm asking you to do is to go into the ring and have one bout. You've been picked for the school team and everyone's depending on you."

"I'll die if you don't get the doctor," Rob suddenly hissed. "Mum!" he shouted.

Mrs. Willison came bounding up the stairs. "What is it, my pet?"

"My stomach hurts. Low down on the right-hand side."

"Appendicitis!" She whirled to face Mr. Willison. "That's what comes of your foolishness!"

"I don't believe it," said Mr. Willison. He went out of the bedroom and down the stairs. The television was still jabbering in the living-room, and for fifteen minutes Mr. Willison forced himself to sit staring at the strident puppets, glistening in the metallic light, as they enacted their Lilliputian rituals. Then he went up to the bedroom again. Mrs. Willison was bathing Rob's forehead.

"His temperature's normal," she said.

"Of course his temperature's normal," said Mr. Willison. "He doesn't want to fight, that's all."

"Fetch the doctor," said a voice from under the cold flannel that swathed Rob's face.

"We will, pet, if you don't get better very soon," said Mrs. Willison, darting a murderous glance at her husband.

* Mr. Willison slowly went downstairs. For a moment he stood looking at the telephone, then picked it up and dialled the number of the grammar school. No

one answered. He replaced the receiver, went to the foot of the stairs and called, "What's the name of the master in charge of this tournament?"

"I don't know," Rob called weakly.

"You told me you'd been training with Mr. Granger," Mr. Willison called. "Would he know anything about it?"

Rob did not answer, so Mr. Willison looked up all the Grangers in the telephone book. There were four in the town, but only one was MA. "That's him," said Mr. Willison. With lead in his heart and ice in his fingers, he dialled the number.

Mrs. Granger fetched Mr. Granger. Yes, he taught at the school. He was the right man. What could he do for Mr. Willison?

"It's about tonight's boxing tournament."

"Sorry, what? The line's bad."

"Tonight's boxing tournament."

"Have you got the right person?"

"You teach my son, Rob—we've just agreed on that. Well, it's about the boxing tournament he's supposed to be taking part in tonight."

"Where?"

"Where? At the school, of course. He's representing the under-fifteens."

There was a pause. "I'm not quite sure what mistake you're making, Mr. Willison, but I think you've got hold of the wrong end of at least one stick." A hearty, defensive laugh. "If Rob belongs to a boxing-club it's certainly news to me, but in any case it can't be anything to do with the school. We don't go in for boxing."

"Don't go in for it?"

"We don't offer it. It's not in our curriculum."

"Oh," said Mr. Willison. "Oh. Thank you. I must have—well, thank you."

"Not at all. I'm glad to answer any queries. Everything's all right, I trust?"

"Oh, yes," said Mr. Willison, "Yes, thanks. Everything's all right."

He put down the telephone, hesitated, then turned and began slowly to climb the stairs.

Two More Endings

On the next page are two more endings to "Manhood," beginning with the passage marked with an asterisk in the story (*"Mr. Willison slowly went downstairs. . . ."). As you read them, consider what readings of manhood might be supported by each ending.

Ending 2

Mr. Willison slowly went downstairs. For a moment he stood looking at the telephone. Then abruptly he turned, shouting up the stairs, "Rob, get out of bed. It's your duty to fight; your duty to your school, to your parents and to yourself." He entered Rob's room and knelt by his bed, speaking quietly. "Everyone's afraid some time, son, but a man faces up to his fears and overcomes them. That's what it means to be a man. Now come on lad, get up." Rob's eyes flickered across to where his mother stood, anxiously wringing her hands, and back to his father. Then he stood up slowly.

Rob's opponent in the ring was Benny Crump, a large, muscular boy, who grinned derisively at Rob and waved confidently to supporters in the crowd. Mr. Willison watched as Rob, pale and nervous, walked to the centre of the ring, listened, nodding, to the referee and then touched gloves with his opponent, before returning to his corner. The bell rang and Rob moved awkwardly forward, his fists up. Benny Crump, ducking and weaving, jabbed at Rob's upraised gloves, feinted with his left and then threw a strong right hook, which hit Rob's guard with such force that he was hit in the face by his own glove. There was laughter from the spectators and a cry rang out, "You're meant to hit the other feller, not yourself, lad."

Mr. Willison flushed angrily and called, "Come on, Rob."

Rob, looking miserable, turned to face a confident Benny Crump, who danced lightly on his toes in front of him and then tapped Rob playfully on each shoulder before hitting him powerfully on the nose. Rob sat down. The audience groaned. "Get 'im off," cried a voice.

The second round was no less painful for Rob or Mr. Willison. Benny skipped about

Ending 3

Mr. Willison slowly went downstairs. For a moment he stood looking at the telephone. Then he dialled the doctor's number.

Rob lay back in bed against a mountain of freshly plumped pillows. His mother fussed about him, tidying needlessly and retucking the corners, pausing every now and then to stroke her son's forehead.

"Would you like something else to eat, dear?" she asked. "The doctor did say you should eat well, remember."

This was true. In the absence of finding anything much else to say, Dr. Sharp had resorted to generalities about early nights, a healthy diet, before making his escape from an obviously tense situation between husband and wife.

Mr. Willison had stormed about the house after the doctor had gone, shouting angrily at his wife, "There's absolutely nothing wrong with the boy. He'll never grow up if you go on mollycoddling him the way you do."

Mrs. Willison didn't answer.

Rob started as his father entered his room. Mr. Willison's eyes took in the heater, the extra pillows and the remains of a very good afternoon tea by the bed. He sighed, and then with an effort said, "Feeling better then, eh lad?" Rob didn't answer, and Mr. Willison continued, "Bad luck falling ill like that, but we'll soon have you back on your feet son and then we'll show 'em a thing or two, won't we lad?

Rob's fingers plucked at the bedspread and he avoided his father's gaze.

"Won't we, lad?" repeated Mr. Willison more insistently, moving closer to the bed and staring down at his son.

the ring, even waving to the spectators at times. Rob looked not to be even trying. With only a minute to go of the round, Mr. Willison stood up and slowly began to walk towards the exit. Rob watched him go, apparently unaware of the punches being landed on him. Mr. Willison felt at that moment a disappointment in his son that was deeper than almost any emotion he'd experienced previously. Rob, at the same time, was feeling an anger quite unlike anything he'd ever felt before. He struck out with all the rage and resentment his father's departure had focussed within him. Benny went down and stayed down. In a daze, Rob heard the count, felt his arm hauled above his head by the referee, and saw his father, face beaming, struggling now through the crowd towards him.

"Well done, Rob, well done!"

The two men shook hands.

"Dad . . . ," mumbled Rob, trying and failing yet again to tell his father the truth about himself, knowing that he couldn't or wouldn't understand. Only his mother knew how much he wanted to dance; that he couldn't remember a time when he hadn't wanted to dance. Rob made an effort to look at his father. Now that he had the chance of a place at the ballet school, there wasn't anything or anybody who was going to stand in his way. Not even if he had to live a lie to do it. He straightened his shoulders and stared back at his father.

"Yes, Dad, we'll show them a thing or two," he answered firmly.

Being a Man

■ In your group, decide which of the following assertions about what it is to be a man could be argued to be promoted by (a) "Manhood" by John Wain, and (b) endings two and three.

Being a man means:	Ending		
	1	2	3
being able to fight.			
being good at sports.			
being able to stand up for yourself.			
being an individual.			
being able to behave in "feminine" ways.			
different things in different cultures and at different times.			
not behaving in ways that are considered "unmanly."			
having sons.			
being successful at work.			
being close to your mother.			
proving that you are not a woman.			

■ Now go through the list again, substituting "woman" in place of "man" and swapping gender references when they occur. Discuss how "appropriate" the assertions seem to be with regard to "womanhood."

For Discussion

■ In your group, discuss the questions which follow the argument below:

"Manhood" seems to start out as a story that encourages debate about different readings of manhood or versions of masculinity. By the end of the story, those debates seem to have taken the form of promoting Rob's right to be himself and to be able to choose—apparently freely—to live his life in the way he wants.

1. Can Rob be an "individual," or is his choice from among different readings of manhood?
2. Is an individuality that is not gendered possible?
3. What versions of masculinity *and* femininity appear to be promoted by "Manhood"?

"Debut"

Kristin Hunter's story "Debut" was published in 1968 in a collection called *Guests in the Promised Land.* In many cultures, a debut signals a young woman's entry into society, with the occasion being marked by a formal dance or ball. Traditionally, it was seen as a chance for affluent families to show off their daughters in the hope that they would attract a suitable young man as a prospective marriage partner. Judy, the character making her debut in this story, however, is from a poor, black family; her right to attend the ball has been won only through the determined efforts of her mother.

Debut

Kristin Hunter

"Hold *still,* Judy," Mrs. Simmons said around the spray of pins that protruded dangerously from her mouth. She gave the thirtieth tug to the tight sash at the waist of the dress. "Now walk over there and turn around slowly."

The dress, Judy's first long one, was white organdie over taffeta, with spaghetti straps that bared her round brown shoulders and a floating skirt and a wide sash that cascaded in a butterfly effect behind. It was a dream, but Judy was sick and tired of the endless fittings she had endured so that she might wear it at the Debutantes' Ball. Her thoughts leaped ahead to the Ball itself . . .

"*Slowly,* I said!" Mrs. Simmons' dark, angular face was always grim, but now it was screwed into an expression resembling a prune. Judy, starting nervously, began to revolve by moving her feet an inch at a time.

Her mother watched her critically. "No, it's still not right. I'll just have to rip out that waistline seam again."

"Oh, Mother!" Judy's impatience slipped out at last. "Nobody's going to notice all those little details."

"They will too. They'll be watching you every minute, hoping to see something wrong. You've got to be the *best*. Can't you get that through your head?" Mrs. Simmons gave a sigh of despair. "You better start noticin' 'all those little details' yourself. I can't do it for you all your life. Now turn around and stand up straight."

"Oh, Mother," close to tears from being made to turn and pose while her feet itched to be dancing, "I can't stand it any more!"

"You can't stand it, huh? How do you think *I* feel?" Mrs. Simmons said in her harshest tone.

Judy was immediately ashamed, remembering the weeks her mother had spent at the sewing machine, pricking her already tattered fingers with needles and pins, and the great weight of sacrifice that had been borne on Mrs. Simmons' shoulders for the past two years so that Judy might bare hers at the Ball.

"All right, take it off," her mother said. "I'm going to take it up the street to Mrs. Luby and let her help me. It's got to be just right or I won't let you leave the house."

"Can't we just leave it the way it is, Mother?" Judy pleaded without hope of success. "I think it's perfect."

"You would," Mrs. Simmons said tartly as she folded the dress and prepared to bear it out of the room. "Sometimes I think I'll never get it through your head. You got to look just right and act just right. That Rose Griffin and those other girls can afford to be careless, maybe, but you can't. You're gonna be the darkest, poorest one there."

Judy shivered in her new lace strapless bra and her old, childish knit snuggies. "You make it sound like a battle I'm going to instead of just a dance."

"It is a battle," her mother said firmly. "It starts tonight and it goes on for the rest of your life. The battle to hold your head up and get someplace and be somebody. We've done all we can for you, your father and I. Now you've got to start fighting some on your own." She gave Judy a slight smile; her voice softened a little. "You'll do all right, don't worry. Try and get some rest this afternoon. Just don't mess up your hair."

"All right, Mother," Judy said listlessly.

She did not really think her father had much to do with anything that happened to her. It was her mother who had ingratiated her way into the Gay Charmers two years ago, taking all sorts of humiliation from the better-dressed, better-off, lighter-skinned women, humbly making and mending their dresses, fixing food for their meetings, addressing more mail and selling more tickets than anyone else. The club had put it off as long as they could, but finally they had to admit Mrs. Simmons to membership because she worked so hard. And that meant, of course, that Judy would be on the list for this year's Ball.

Her father, a quiet carpenter who had given up any other ambitions years ago, did not think much of society or his wife's fierce determination to launch Judy into it. "Just keep clean and be decent," he would say. "That's all anybody has to do."

Her mother always answered, "If that's all *I* did we'd still be on relief," and he would shut up with shame over the years when he had been laid off repeatedly and her days' work and sewing had kept them going. Now he had steady work but she refused to quit, as if she expected it to end at any moment. The intense energy that burned in Mrs. Simmons' large dark eyes had scorched her features in permanent irony. She worked day and night and spent her spare time scheming and planning. Whatever her personal ambitions had been, Judy knew she blamed Mr. Simmons for their failure; now all her schemes revolved around their only child.

Judy went to her mother's window and watched her stride down the street with the dress until she was hidden by the high brick wall that went around two sides of their house. Then she returned to her own room. She did not get dressed because she was afraid of pulling a sweater over her hair—her mother would notice the difference even if it looked all right to Judy—and because she was afraid that doing anything, even getting dressed, might precipitate her into battle. She drew a stool up to her window and looked out. She had no real view, but she liked her room. The wall hid the crowded tenement houses beyond the alley, and from its cracks and bumps and depressions she could construct any imaginary landscape she chose. It was how she had spent most of the free hours of her dreamy adolescence.

"Hey, can I go?"

It was the voice of an invisible boy in the alley. As another boy chuckled, Judy recognised the familiar ritual; if you said yes, they said, "Can I go with you?" It had been tried on her dozens of times. She always walked past, head in the air, as if she had not heard. Her mother said that was the only thing to do; if they knew she was a lady, they wouldn't dare bother her. But this time a girl's voice, cool and assured, answered.

"If you think you're big enough," it said.

It was Lucy Mae Watkins; Judy could picture her standing there in a tight dress with bright, brazen eyes.

"I'm big enough to give you a baby," the boy answered.

Judy would die if a boy ever spoke to her like that, but she knew Lucy Mae could handle it. Lucy Mae could handle all the boys, even if they ganged up on her, because she had been born knowing something other girls had to learn.

"Aw, you ain't big enough to give me a shoe-shine," she told him.

"Come here and I'll show you how big I am," the boy said.

"Yeah, Lucy Mae, what's happenin'?" another boy said. "Come here and tell us."

Lucy Mae laughed. "What I'm puttin' down is too strong for little boys like you."

"Come here a minute, baby," the first boy said. "I got a cigarette for you."

"Aw, I ain't studyin' your cigarettes," Lucy Mae answered. But her voice was closer, directly below Judy. There were the sounds of a scuffle and Lucy Mae's muffled laughter. When she spoke her voice sounded raw and cross. "Come on now, boy. Cut it out and give me the damn cigarette." There was more scuffling, and the sharp crack of a slap, and then Lucy Mae said, "Cut it out, I said. Just for that I'm gonna take 'em all." The clack of high heels rang down the sidewalk with a boy's clumsy shoes in pursuit.

Judy realised that there were three of them down there. "Let her go, Buster," one said. "You can't catch her now."

"Aw, hell, man, she took the whole damn pack," the one called Buster complained.

"That'll learn you!" Lucy Mae's voice mocked from down the street. "Don't mess with nothin' you can't handle."

"Hey, Lucy Mae. Hey, I heard Rudy Grant already gave you a baby," a second boy called out.

"Yeah. Is that true, Lucy Mae?" the youngest one yelled.

There was no answer. She must be a block away by now.

For a moment the hidden boys were silent; then one of them guffawed directly below Judy, and the other two joined in the secret male laughter that was oddly high-pitched and feminine.

"Aw man, I don't know what you all laughin' about," Buster finally grumbled. "That girl took all my cigarettes. You got some Leroy?"

"Naw," the second boy said.

"What we gonna do? I ain't got but fifteen cents. Hell, man, I want more than a feel for a packet of cigarettes." There was an unpleasant whine in Buster's voice. "Hell, for a pack of cigarettes I want a girl to come across."

"She will next time," Buster said. "You know she better. If she pass by here again, we gonna jump her, you hear?"

"Sure, man," Leroy said. "The three of us can grab her easy."

"Then we can all three of us have some fun. Oh, *yeah*, man," the youngest boy said. He sounded as if he might be about fourteen.

Leroy said, "We oughta get Roland and J. T. too. For a whole pack of cigarettes she oughta treat all five of us."

"Aw, man, why tell Roland and J. T.?" the youngest voice whined. "They ain't in it. Them was *our* cigarettes."

"They was *my* cigarettes, you mean," Buster said with authority. "You guys better quit it before I decide to cut you out."

"Oh, man, don't do that. We with you. You know that."

"Sure, man, we your aces, man."

"All right, that's better." There was a minute of silence.

Then, "What we gonna do with the girl, Buster?" the youngest one wanted to know.

"When she come back we gonna jump her, man. We gonna jump her and grab her. Then we gonna turn her every way but loose." He went on, spinning a crude fantasy that got wilder each time he retold it, until it became so secretive that their voices dropped to a low indistinct murmur punctuated by guffaws. Now and then Judy could distinguish the word "girl" or the other word they used for it; these words always produced the loudest guffaws of all. She shook off her fear with the thought that Lucy Mae was too smart to pass there again today. She had heard them at their dirty talk in the alley before and had always been successful in ignoring it; it had nothing to do with her, the wall protected her from their kind. All the ugliness was on their side of it, and this side was hers to fill with beauty.

She turned on her radio to shut them out completely and began to weave her tapestry to its music. More for practice than anything else, she started by picturing the maps of the places to which she intended to travel, then went on to the faces of her friends. Rose Griffin's sharp, Indian profile appeared on the wall. Her colouring was Indian too and her hair was straight and black and glossy. Judy's hair, naturally none of these things, had been "done" four days ago so that tonight it would be "old" enough to have a gloss as natural-looking as Rose's. But Rose, despite her handsome looks, was silly; her voice broke constantly into high-pitched giggles and she became even sillier and more nervous around boys.

Judy was not sure that she knew how to act around boys either. The sister kept boys and girls apart at the Catholic high school where her parents sent her to keep her away from low-class kids. But she felt that she knew a secret: tonight, in that dress, with her hair in a sophisticated upswept, she would be transformed into a poised princess. Tonight all the college boys her mother described so eagerly would rush to dance with her, and then from somewhere *the boy* would appear. She did not know his name; she neither knew nor cared whether he went to college, but she imagined that he would be as dark as she was, and that there would be awe and diffidence in his manner as he bent to kiss her hand . . .

A waltz swelled from the radio; the wall, turning blue in deepening twilight, came alive with whirling figures. Judy rose and began to go through the steps she had rehearsed for so many weeks. She swirled with a practised smile on her face, holding an imaginary skirt at her side; turned, dipped, and flicked on her bedside lamp without missing a fraction of the beat. Faster and faster she danced with her imaginary partner, to an inner music that was better than the sounds on the radio. She was "coming out," and tonight the world would discover what it had been waiting for all these years.

"Aw git it, baby." She ignored it as she would ignore the crowds lining the streets to watch her pass on her way to the Ball.

"Aw, do your number." She waltzed on, safe and secure on her side of the wall.

"Can I come up there and do it with you?"

At this she stopped, paralysed. Somehow they had come over the wall or around it and into her road.

"Man, I sure like the view from here," the youngest boy said. "How come we never tried this view before."

She came to life, ran quickly to the lamp and turned it off, but not before Buster said, "Yeah, and the back view is fine, too."

"Aw, she turned off the light," a voice complained.

"Put it on again, baby, we don't mean no harm."

"Let us see you dance some more. I bet you can really do it."

"Yeah, I bet she can shimmy on down."

"You know it man."

"Come on down here, baby," Buster's voice urged softly, dangerously. "I got a cigarette for you."

"Yeah, and he got something else for you, too."

Judy, flattened against her closet door, gradually lost her urge to scream. She realised that she was shivering in her underwear. Taking a deep breath, she opened the closet door and found her robe. She thought of going to the window and yelling down, "You don't have anything I want. Do you understand?" But she had more important things to do.

Wrapping her hair in a protective plastic, she ran a full steaming tub and dumped in half a bottle of her mother's favourite cologne. At first she scrubbed herself furiously, irritating her skin. But finally she stopped, knowing she would never be able to get cleaner than this again.

She could not wash away the thing they considered dirty, the thing that made them pronounce "girl" in the same way as the other four-letter words they wrote on the wall in the alley; it was part of her, just as it was part of her mother and Rose Griffin and Lucy Mae. She relaxed then because it was true that the boys in the alley did not have a thing she wanted. She had what they wanted, and the knowledge replaced her shame with a strange, calm feeling of power.

After her bath she splashed on more cologne and spent forty minutes on her make-up, erasing and retracing her eyebrows six times until she was satisfied. She went to her mother's room then and found the dress, finished and freshly pressed, on its hanger.

When Mrs. Simmons came upstairs to help her daughter she found her sitting on the bench before the vanity mirror as if it were a throne. She looked young and arrogant and beautiful and perfect and cold.

"Why, you're dressed already," Mrs. Simmons said in surprise. While she stared, Judy rose with perfect, icy grace and glided to the centre of the room. She stood there motionless as a mannequin.

"I want you to fix the hem, Mother," she directed. "It's still uneven at the back."

Her mother went down obediently on her knees muttering, "It looks all right to me." She put in a couple of pins. "That better?"

"Yes," Judy said with a brief glance at the mirror. "You'll have to sew it on me, Mother. I can't take it off now. I'd ruin my hair."

Mrs. Simmons went to fetch her sewing things, returned and surveyed her daughter. "You sure did a good job on yourself, I must say," she admitted grudgingly. "Can't find a thing to complain about. You'll look as good as anybody there."

"Of course, Mother," Judy said as Mrs. Simmons knelt and sewed. "I don't know what you were so worried about." Her secret feeling of confidence had returned, stronger than ever, but the evening ahead was no longer a girlish fantasy she had pictured on the wall; it had hard, clear outlines leading up to a definite goal. She would be the belle of the Ball because she knew more than Rose Griffin and her silly friends; more than her mother, more, even than Lucy Mae, because she knew better than to settle for a mere pack of cigarettes.

"There," her mother said, breaking the thread. She got up. "I never expected to get you ready this early. Ernest Lee won't be here for another hour."

"That silly Ernest Lee," Judy said, with a new contempt in her young voice. Until tonight she had been pleased by the thought of going to the dance with Ernest Lee; he was nice, she felt comfortable with him, and he might even be the awe-struck boy of her dream. He was a dark, serious neighbourhood boy who could not afford to go to college; Mrs. Simmons had reluctantly selected him to take Judy to the dance because all the Gay Charmers' sons were spoken for. Now, with an undertone of excitement, Judy said, "I'm going to ditch him after the dance, Mother. You'll see. I'm going to come home with one of the college boys."

"It's very nice, Ernest Lee," she told him an hour later when he handed her the white orchid, "but it's rather small. I'm going to wear it on my wrist, if you don't mind." And then, dazzling him with a smile of sweetest cruelty, she stepped back and waited while he fumbled with the door.

"You know, Edward, I'm not worried about her any more," Mrs. Simmons said to her husband after the children were gone. Her voice became harsh and grating. "Put down that paper and listen to me! Aren't you interested in your child?—That's better," she said as he complied meekly. "I was saying, I do believe she's learned what I've been trying to teach her, after all."

Reading Character

A reading practice which views characters in stories as "real people" might ask readers the following question: What kinds of people are Mr. and Mrs. Simmons, Judy, Lucy Mae, the boys in the alley, and Ernest Lee?

- Divide your page into five columns and head them with each of the names mentioned in the question. Then, in pairs, write down about four words or brief phrases to describe each one. Compare and discuss your completed lists with the other pair in your group.

- In a class discussion, share your lists and talk about similarities and differences in them. Is there any consensus in terms of which characters are described most positively or negatively?

How and Why Are Particular Readings Produced?

The words you were asked to compile to "describe" each of the characters were, of course, readings of the characters. That is, as a reader, you produced different readings of the characters mentioned, by assigning certain sets of meanings to them.

It used to be thought that readers constructed readings of characters by paying attention to: (a) what characters do and say; (b) what other characters say about them; (c) description of characters' interior thoughts and feelings; and (d) direct description by the writer.

This view implies that what is said and done by characters gives readers access to an understanding of what the character is "like." Often, however, the *same* behaviour is read very differently by readers, depending on the sex, class, or race of the characters. These differences arise because the textual construction of characters is always fragmentary and readers fill gaps with already available readings.

Filling Gaps

The readings available to fill gaps in the construction of, for example, the boys in the alley and Lucy Mae, can be argued to differ, not because they describe what these different characters are "like," but rather, because of differences in dominant readings of gender. Readings of boys who are reputed to be sexually active, or would like to be, tend to differ from readings of girls who are thought to act in similar ways.

It can be argued that readers do not just build up a picture of what a character is like, from what they say and do, but rather that readers reproduce already available readings which are activated by particular sets of words. These sets of words activate or "trigger" readings that readers recognize and use to fill gaps in the text. For example, this next following set of words enables readers to construct a particular reading of Lucy Mae:

> ". . . standing there in a tight dress with bright brazen eyes."

- Discuss the effect the following substitutions appear to have on the readings produced.

> ". . . standing there in a patched dress with bright eager eyes."
> ". . . standing there in a starched dress with shining courageous eyes."
> ". . . standing there in a baggy dress with bold cheerful eyes."

- Try substituting other words such as "tailored" for "tight"; "suit" or "trousers" for "dress"; and "shameless" for "brazen."
- As a class, discuss how different meanings or readings appear to be produced and assigned to characters, and why they might differ, in the ways that they appear to in this activity.

Versions of Masculinity and Femininity

Below is a way to think about characters in "Debut" as particular versions or readings of masculinity and femininity:

- With a partner, consider how you might describe each of the characters listed below, in terms of the trait pairs listed on the right. Record a number from each pair of opposites for each character, indicating any qualifications that you might want to make. For example, many readers read Lucy Mae as 1, 3, 5 (she is "outside," while Judy doesn't leave the apartment until the end of the story), and 7, but then cannot decide between 9 and 10.

Versions of Femininity and Masculinity		
Femininity	**Trait Numbers**	**Pairs of Opposite Traits**
Judy (before the incident with the boys)		1 Strong or 2 Weak
Mrs. Simmons		
Lucy Mae		3 Active or 4 Passive
Judy (after the incident with the boys)		
		5 Public or 6 Private
Masculinity		
Mr. Simmons		7 Mobile or 8 Static
Boys in the alley		
Ernest Lee		9 Rational or 10 Emotional

- Compare your list of numbers for each character with those of another pair. Then, for each character, record whether you have assigned them mainly odd or mainly even numbers.
- In dominant readings of gender, which characters, would you argue, might be the most admired and the least admired versions of femininity and masculinity?
- Swap Judy's first set of numbers with Mr. Simmons's numbers. Decide which would be the most admired and least admired now.
- In a class discussion, share your decisions and comment on the degree of consensus or lack of it.

Doing What Comes Naturally?

- In your group, discuss how likely or unlikely a financially secure and successful life might be for the characters listed below if they follow Mr. Simmons's adage to "Just keep clean and be decent." That is, if the social position of the characters mentioned doesn't change, what might you predict their future prospects to be? You could set out your decisions in the form of a chart as shown below:

Chances of Being Financially Secure and Successful				
	Unlikely	**Possible**	**Likely**	**Very Likely**
Gay Charmers' sons				
Gay Charmers' daughters				
Lucy Mae				
Boys in the alley				
Judy				
Ernest Lee				

- Discuss how any of the above characters might ensure or improve their chances of a secure and successful life. Which of those characters might incur negative readings by attempting to make such improvements?

References

Barnard, Marjorie. "The Lottery." *The Persimmon Tree and Other Stories.* New York: Penguin, 1986.

Brautigan, Richard. "The Scarlatti Tilt." *Revenge of the Lawn: Stories, 1962–1970.* New York: Simon, 1971.

Gibbs, Angelica. "The Test." *New Yorker* 15 June 1940.

Grace, Patricia. "A Way of Talking." *Waiariki and Other Stories.* 1975. New York: Penguin, 1986.

Head, Bessie. "Looking for a Rain God." *The Collector of Treasures and Other Botswana Village Tales.* African Writers Series. 1977. Oxford: Heinemann, 1992.

Hunter, Kristin. "Debut." *Guests in the Promised Land: Stories.* New York: Scribner, 1973.

Hunter, Tony. "Listen to the End." *The Hat Trick: Australian Short Stories.* Ed. Michael Dugan, Barbara Giles, and J. S. Hamilton. Kew, Victoria, Australia: Fellowship of Australian Writers in association with Broken Hill Proprietary Co. Ltd., 1981.

Kurosaka, R. T. "A Lot to Learn." *The Little Book of Horrors.* Ed. Sebastian Wolfe. New York: Barricade, 1992.

Morehead, Sheila. "At Seventeen." *The Hat Trick: Australian Short Stories.* Ed. Michael Dugan, Barbara Giles, and J. S. Hamilton. Kew, Victoria, Australia: Fellowship of Australian Writers in association with Broken Hill Proprietary Co. Ltd., 1981.

Oates, Joyce Carol. "How I Contemplated the World from the Detroit House of Correction and Began My Life Over Again." *Where Are You Going, Where Have You Been?: Selected Early Stories.* New York: Ontario Review Press, 1993.

Wain, John. "Manhood." *Death of the Hind Legs, and Other Stories.* New York: Viking, 1966.

Winton, Tim. "A Blow, a Kiss." *Scission.* New York: Penguin, 1985.

About the Authors

Bronwyn Mellor holds a doctorate in education and English from the University of Western Australia. She is the publisher and editorial director of Chalkface Press, which she co-founded in 1987 on returning to Australia from Britain. She taught English in secondary schools in England and worked as a contributory writer and advisory teacher at the English and Media Centre in London. She has also taught in secondary schools in Australia and lectured in university courses in curriculum and English studies.

Annette Patterson teaches sociology and English in the School of Education at James Cook University, Townsville, Queensland, Australia. Previously, she taught English and literature in high schools from 1976–1989. She also has worked as a member of the Chalkface Press writing team to produce texts for secondary English students. Her research interests include critical reading practices and histories of English education. Her book *Questions of English*, written with Robin Peel and Jeanne Gerlach, is forthcoming from Routledge Press. Currently, she is working on a history of reading instruction from the sixteenth century.

Marnie O'Neill is a senior lecturer at the University of Western Australia in the areas of English education, language literacy and learning, and teaching and learning. Her research interests include English curriculum studies, curriculum policy and practice, language in education, teaching and learning, classroom studies, gender studies, and gifted and talented education. She has also been a secondary school English teacher, an advisory teacher in English, a chief examiner in English and literature, and, for some years, the editor of the journal of the Australian Association for the Teaching of English, *English in Australia*. The writer of numerous papers, articles, and books, she has co-written texts for secondary students published by Chalkface Press.

This book was typeset in AGaramond by Electronic Imaging.
The typefaces used on the cover were AGaramond, Helvetica Narrow, and Trajan.
The book was printed on 60-lb. Finch Opaque by IPC Communication Services.